Sco

THE
HIGHLAND
CLEARANCES

Scottish Histories

The Highland Clearances

Adapted from the writings of
Alexander McKenzie

WAVERLEY
BOOKS

This edition published 2008 by Geddes & Grosset,
David Dale House, New Lanark ML11 9DJ, Scotland

© 2001 Geddes & Grosset

ISBN 978 1 902407 67 8

Printed and bound in India

CONTENTS

CHAPTER I

SUTHERLAND

The Sutherland Clearances

To give a proper account of the Sutherland Clearances would take a bulky volume. Indeed, a large work, called *An Account of the Sutherland Improvements*, has been written and published in their defence by James Loch, the Commissioner for the Marchioness of Stafford and heiress of Sutherland, and the man who was mainly responsible for the Clearances. This was the first account I ever read of these so-called improvements. It convinced me that the 'improvement' of the people, by driving them in the most merciless and cruel manner from the homes of their fathers, was carried out on a huge scale and in the most inconsiderate and heartless manner by those in charge of the Sutherland estates. But when one reads the other side, such as Macleod's *Gloomy Memories* and General Stewart of Garth's *Sketches of the Highlanders*, one wonders that such iniquities could ever have been permitted in any Christian country.

The landlords, generally led by southern factors worse than themselves, were, in most cases, motivated by pure self-interest, and they pursued their policy of extermination with a recklessness and remorselessness unparalleled anywhere else where the Gospel of peace and charity was preached – except, perhaps, Ireland. Generally, law and justice, religion and humanity, were either totally disregarded, or, worse, were used as instruments of oppression. Every conceivable means, short of the musket and the sword, were used to drive the natives from the land they loved, and to force them to exchange their crofts and homes – originally built by themselves or their forefathers

– for wretched patches among the barren rocks on the seashore. There they had to depend, after losing their livestock and having their houses destroyed, on the uncertain produce of the sea for subsistence. This was difficult for the people, especially those in Sutherland, as they were unfamiliar with a seafaring life and its dangers.

What was true generally of the Highlands was in Sutherland carried to the greatest extreme. That unfortunate county, according to an eye-witness, was made another Moscow. The inhabitants were burned out, and every contrivance and ingenious and unrelenting cruelty was eagerly adopted to remove the people. Many lives were lost to famine, hardship and deprivation; hundreds, stripped of their all, emigrated to Canada and other parts of America. Great numbers, especially of the young, sought employment in the Lowlands and in England, where, as few of them were skilled workmen, they were obliged – even farmers who had lived in comparative affluence in their own country – to compete with common labourers in communities where their language and simple manners made them figures of fun. The aged and infirm, the widows and orphans, and others who were tied to the soil of their ancestors, were induced to accept poor allotments on the wild moors and barren rocks. The mild nature and religious upbringing of the Highlanders prevented them from the sort of determined resistance and revenge which limited the greed of landlords in Ireland. Their ignorance of the English language and the want of natural leaders made it impossible for them to broadcast their grievances. They were, therefore, maltreated with impunity. The clergy generally sided with the oppressing lairds, who were patrons of the church, sanctioning the iniquity: 'the foulest deeds were glossed over, and all the evil which could not be attributed to the natives themselves, such as severe seasons, famines and consequent disease, was by these pious gentlemen ascribed to Providence, as a punishment for sin'.

The evictions carried out in the Highlands during the early nineteenth century were more severe and cruel in Sutherland than in any other region. The Countess-Marchioness and her husband, the Marquis of Stafford, were by no means lacking in humanity but atrocious acts were carried out in their name by heartless underlings, who represented the tenants to their superiors as lazy and rebellious. Countrymen from the South were introduced and the land given to them for sheep farms over the heads of the native tenantry. These strangers were made justices of the peace and armed with all sorts of authority which enabled them to act in the most tyrannical fashion; the tenants were completely at their mercy. They dared not complain, for their oppressors were also the administrators of the law.

The Sutherland Clearances began in a comparatively mild way in 1807, with the ejection of ninety families from Farr and Lairg. They were provided with smaller lots, fifteen or seventeen miles away, to which they were permitted to remove their cattle and furnishings, leaving their crops unprotected in the ground from which they were evicted. They had to pull down their old houses, remove the timber and build new ones, often having to sleep in the open in the meantime. In the autumn they carried away what remained of their crops but the exhausting effort required resulted in illness for many and death for some.

In 1809 several hundred were evicted from the parishes of Dornoch, Rogart, Loth, Clyne and Golspie, under circumstances of much greater severity. Several were driven by various means to leave the country altogether. Those who could not be persuaded to do so were offered patches of moor and bog off Dornoch Moor and Brora Links which were unfit for cultivation. This process was carried on annually until, in 1811, the land from which the people were ejected was divided into large farms and advertised as huge sheep runs. The country was overrun with strangers who came to look at these extensive tracts. Some of these gentlemen complained of threats from the evicted tenantry. A rumour spread that one of the interlopers was pursued and threatened by some of the natives of Kildonan. The 21st Regiment was marched from Fort George to Dunrobin Castle, with artillery and ammunition. A great farce was performed; the people were summoned by the factors to the castle at a certain hour. They came peaceably but the riot act was read; a few sheepish, innocent Highlanders were made prisoners, but were almost immediately released without charge, while the soldiers were ordered back to Fort George. The demonstration, however, had the desired effect of cowing the people into absolute submission. The clergy, meanwhile, preached that the vengeance of Heaven and eternal damnation would fall on all those who would resist. In May 1812, large districts of these parishes were cleared peacefully, the poor creatures believing the false teaching of their dishonest spiritual guides! The Earl of Selkirk, who went personally to the district, persuaded many of those evicted to emigrate to his estates on the Red River in British North America. After a terrible passage, they found left in a wilderness in a strange climate, with no protection from the native people, who plundered them on their arrival and finally massacred them. The few who managed to escape travelled, through immense difficulties, across trackless forests to Upper Canada.

In the spring of 1814, the notorious Mr. Sellar, at this time sub-factor, took a large portion of the parishes of Farr and Kildonan into his own hands. In the month of March, the old tenantry received notices to quit the following May. A few days after the summonses were served, most of the heath pasture was, on Sellar's orders, set on fire. Thus, the cattle belonging to the old tenantry, dependent on the grass sprouting among the heather for subsistence during the spring, were left without food and it was impossible to sell them at a fair price. To make matters worse, fodder was unusually scarce this year.

In May, evictions began again, accompanied by cruelties hitherto unknown, as described in the following eye-witness account:

'In former removals the tenants had been allowed to carry away the timber of their old dwellings to erect houses on their new allotments, but now a more summary mode was adopted by setting fire to them. The able-bodied men were at this time away after their cattle or otherwise engaged elsewhere. Those who suffered first from the general house-burning that now began were the aged and infirm, the women and children. As the lands were now in the hands of the factor himself, and were to be occupied as sheep farms, and as the people made no resistance, they expected at least to be allowed to occupy their houses and other buildings till they could gradually

10

move, and meanwhile look after their growing crops. Their consternation was therefore greater when a move was made to pull down
and burn the houses over their heads. The old people, women and
others began to preserve the timber which was their own; but the
devastators continued, speedily demolishing all before them and, when
they had overthrown all the houses in a large tract of country, they
set fire to the remains. Timber, furniture and every other article that
could not be instantly removed was utterly destroyed. The proceedings were carried on with the greatest speed and cruelty. The cries of
the victims, the confusion, the despair and horror painted on the
countenances of the one party, and the exulting ferocity of the other,
beggar all description. At these scenes Mr. Sellar was present and,
apparently, as sworn by several witnesses at his subsequent trial, ordering and directing the whole. Many deaths ensued from alarm,
from fatigue and cold, the people having been instantly deprived of
shelter and left to the mercies of the elements. Some old men took to
the woods and to the rocks, wandering about in a state close to in-
sanity and several of them in this situation lived only a few days.
Pregnant women were taken in premature labour and several children did not survive.

'To these scenes,' says Donald Macleod, 'I was an eye-witness, and
am ready to substantiate the truth of my statements, not only by my
own testimony, but by that of many others who were present at the
time. In such a scene of general devastation, it is almost useless to
describe individual cases; the suffering was universal. I shall, however,
mention a few of the extreme cases I witnessed. John Mackay's wife,
Ravigill, in attempting to pull down her house in the absence of her
husband, to preserve the timber, fell through the roof. As a result she
went into premature labour, in the open air and in view of all by-
standers. Donald Munro, Garvott, lying in a fever, was turned out of
his house and exposed to the elements. Donald Macbeath, an infirm
and bed-ridden old man, had the house unroofed over him, and sub-
sequently died from his exposure. I was present at the pulling down
and burning of the house of William Chisholm, Badinloskin, in which
was lying his wife's mother, an old bed-ridden woman of nearly 100

11

years of age, alone. I persuaded the people about to set fire to the house to wait until Mr. Sellar came. On his arrival, I told him of the poor old woman being in a condition unfit for removal, and he replied, "Damn her, the old witch, she has lived too long – let her burn." Fire was immediately set to the house, and the blankets in which she was carried out were in flames before she could be got out. She was placed in a little shed, and it was with great difficulty they were prevented from firing it also. The old woman's daughter arrived while the house was on fire and helped the neighbours move her mother out of the flames and smoke, presenting a picture of horror which I shall never forget, but cannot attempt to describe. Within five days she was a corpse.'

In 1816, Sellar was charged at Inverness, before the Court of Justiciary, with culpable homicide and fire raising in connection with these proceedings, but was 'honourably' acquitted. Almost immediately after, however, he ceased to be factor on the Sutherland estates and Mr. Loch came into power. Evictions were carried out from 1814 to 1820, similar to those already described, but the removal of Mr. Young, the chief factor, and Mr. Sellar from power was hailed with delight by the remaining population. Their appearance in any part of the county caused such alarm as to make women hysterical. One woman became insane with fear and, whenever she saw anyone she did not recognize, she cried out in terror, '*Oh! sin Sellar*' – 'Oh! there's Sellar.' However, the new factors were not much better. Several current leases would not expire until 1819 or 1820, so that the evictions were only partial from 1814 until then. The people were reduced to such a state of poverty that even Mr. Loch himself, in his *Sutherland Improvements*, admits that 'Their wretchedness was so great that, after pawning everything they possessed to the fishermen on the coast, such as had no cattle were reduced to come down from the hills in hundreds for the purpose of gathering cockles on the shore. Those who lived in the more remote situations of the county were obliged to subsist upon broth made of nettles, thickened with a little oatmeal. Those who had cattle had recourse to the still more wretched expedient of bleeding them, and mixing the blood with oatmeal, which they afterwards cut into slices and fried. Those who had a little money came down and slept all night upon the beach, in order to watch the boats returning from the fishing, hoping to obtain a part of what had been caught.' He failed to mention the fact that he had had constables stationed at the Little Ferry to prevent the starved tenantry from collecting shellfish in the only place where they could find them.

He urged the people to sign documents agreeing to move at the next Whitsunday term, promising at the same time to provide for them elsewhere. A month later, the devastation again began, with parts of the parishes of Golspie, Rogart and Farr and the whole of Kildonan set ablaze. Three hundred houses were burned and their occupants pushed out in the open without food or shelter. Macleod, who was present, describes the horrible scene as follows:

'The consternation and confusion were extreme; little or no time was given for the removal of persons or property. The people struggled to remove the sick and the helpless before the fire should reach them and to save the most valuable of their effects. The cries of the women and children, the roaring of the frightened cattle, hunted at the same time by the yelling dogs of the shepherds amid the smoke and fire, presented a scene that defies description – it had to be seen to be believed. A dense cloud of smoke enveloped the whole country by day and even extended far out to sea; at night a terrific scene presented itself – all the houses in an extensive district in flames at once. I myself climbed a hill late in the evening, and counted two hundred and fifty blazing houses, many of the owners of which were my relations, and all of whom I personally knew, but whose present condition I could not tell. The conflagration lasted six days, till all the houses were reduced to smoking ruins. During one of these days a boat actually lost her way in the dense smoke as she approached the shore, but at night was guided to a landing-place by the lurid light of the flames.'

All the inhabitants of Kildonan, numbering nearly 2000, except three families, were utterly rooted and burned out and the whole parish converted into a solitary wilderness. Some lost their reason.

13

Over a hundred souls took passage to Caithness in a small sloop, the master agreeing to take them in the hold, from which he had just unloaded a cargo of quicklime. A storm came on and they were nine days at sea in the most miserable conditions – men, women, and children huddled together, with barely any provisions. Several died and others became invalids for the rest of their days. One man, Donald Mackay, whose family was suffering from a severe fever, carried two of his children twenty-five miles to the ship. Another old man took shelter in a meal mill, where he was kept from starvation by licking the meal refuse scattered among the dust on the floor. George Munro, the miller at Farr, who had six of his family down with fever, had to remove them in that state to a damp kiln while his home was burned.

General Stewart of Garth, about a year after the cruelties perpetrated in Sutherland, writes with regret of the unnatural proceedings as 'the delusions practised [by his subordinates] on a generous and public-spirited proprietor, which have been so perseveringly applied that it would appear as if all feeling of former kindness towards the native tenantry had ceased to exist. To them any uncultivated spot of moorland, however small, was considered enough to support a family while the most lavish encouragement has been given to all the new tenants, on whom, with the erection of buildings, the improvement of lands, roads, bridges, and so on, upwards of £210,000 had been spent since 1808. It cannot be sufficiently lamented that an estimate of the character of these poor people was taken from the misrepresentations of interested persons.' He adds that, if the tenants' proven good character and capabilities had been taken into account, and if they had been permitted to stay and farm the soil under proper management in return for a small share of the benefits, 'such a humane and considerate regard to the prosperity of a whole people would undoubtedly have answered every good purpose.'

In 1828, Donald Macleod, after a considerable absence, returned to his native Kildonan. He attended service in the parish church, where he found a congregation of eight shepherds and their dogs, the minister and three members of his family. Macleod came in too late for the first psalm but, at the end of the service, the fine old tune

Bangor was given out 'when the four-footed hearers became excited, got up on the seats, and raised a most infernal chorus of howling. Their masters attacked them with their crooks, which only made matters worse; the yelping and howling continued to the end of the service.' Donald Macleod retired to contemplate the painful and shameful scene and to contrast it with past experience as a member of the large and devout congregation that had formerly worshipped in the parish church of his native valley.

The Parish Church of Farr no longer existed; the population of Strathnaver was rooted and burned out during the general conflagration and presented a similar aspect to his own native parish. The church was razed to the ground and its timbers taken to construct one of the Sutherland 'improvements', the Inn at Altnaharra, while the minister's house was converted into a dwelling for a fox-hunter. A woman, well-known in the parish, who had travelled through the desolated strath the following year, was asked on her return home for her news. She replied, '*O, chan eil ach sgiala bronach! sgiala bronach!*' 'Oh, only sad news, sad news! I have seen the timber of our well-attended kirk covering the inn at Altnaharra; I have seen the kirkyard where our friends are mouldering filled with tarry sheep and Mr. Sage's study turned into a kennel for Robert Gunn's dogs and I have seen a crow's nest in James Gordon's chimney head,' after which she fell into a paroxysm of grief.

Hugh Miller on the Sutherland Clearances
(From *Sketches of the Highlanders* by General Stewart of Garth)

So much has been already said about these disastrous Sutherland evictions that we fear the reader is sickened with the horrid narrative but, as it is intended to make the present record of these atrocious proceedings as complete as it is now possible to make it, we must place before the reader at considerable length Hugh Miller's observations on this National Crime, especially as his remarks largely embody the philosophical views and conclusions of the able and far-seeing French writer Sismondi, who in his great work declares, 'It is by a cruel use

15

of legal power – it is by an unjust usurpation – that the tacksman and the tenant of Sutherland are considered as having no right to the land which they have occupied for so many ages. . . A count or earl has no more right to expel from their homes the inhabitants of his county, than a king to expel from his country the inhabitants of his kingdom.' Hugh Miller introduces his remarks on Sutherland by a reference to the celebrated Frenchman's work and his opinion of the Sutherland Clearances, thus:

'There appeared in Paris about five years ago a singularly ingenious work on political economy from the pen of the late M. de Sismondi, a writer of European reputation. Most of the first volume is taken up with discussions on territorial wealth and the condition of the cultivators of the soil and, in this part of the work, there is a prominent place assigned to a subject which perhaps few Scottish readers would expect to see introduced through the medium of a foreign language to the people of a great continental state. We find this philosophic writer, whose works are known far beyond the limits of his language, devoting an entire essay to the case of the Duchess of Sutherland and her tenants, and forming a judgment on it very unlike the decision of political economists in our own country, who have not hesitated to characterize her singularly harsh experiment as at once justifiable in itself and happy in its results. It is curious to observe how deeds done as if in darkness and in a corner are beginning, after the lapse of nearly thirty years, to be proclaimed on the house-tops. The experiment of the late Duchess was not intended to be made in the eye of Europe. Its details would ill bear the exposure. When Cobbett simply referred to it, only ten years ago, the noble proprietrix was startled, as if a rather delicate family secret was about to be divulged; and yet nothing seems more evident now than that civilized man all over the world is to be made aware of how the experiment was accomplished and what it is ultimately to produce.

'In a time of quiet and good order, when law, whether in the right or in the wrong, is all potent in enforcing its findings, the argument which the philosophic Frenchman employs on behalf of the ejected tenantry of Sutherland is an argument at which proprietors may afford to smile. In a time of revolution, however, when lands change their owners, and old families give place to new ones, it might be found somewhat formidable – sufficiently so, at least, to lead a wise proprietor in an unsettled age rather to conciliate than to oppress and irritate the class who would be able in such circumstances to urge it with most effect. It is not easy doing justice in a few sentences to the facts and reasonings of an elaborate essay, but the line of argument runs thus:

'Under the old Celtic tenures – the only tenures through which the Lords of Sutherland derive their rights to their lands – the *Klaan,* or children of the soil, were the proprietors of the soil – "the whole of Sutherland," says Sismondi, belonged to "the men of Sutherland." Their chief was their monarch, and a very absolute monarch he was. He gave the different *tacks* of land to his officers or took them away from them, according as they showed themselves more or less useful in war. But, though he could thus, in a military sense, reward or punish the clan, he could not diminish in the least the property of the clan itself – he was a chief, not a proprietor, and had no more right to expel from their homes the inhabitants of his county than a king to expel from his country the inhabitants of his kingdom.

"'Now, the Gaelic tenant," continues the Frenchman, "has never been conquered; nor did he forfeit, on any later occasion, the rights which he originally possessed." In point of right, he is still a co-proprietor with his captain. To a Scotsman acquainted with the law of property as it has existed among us, in even the Highlands, for the last century, and everywhere else for at least two centuries more, the view may seem extreme; not so, however, to a native of the Continent, in many parts of which prescription and custom are found ranged not on the side of the chief but on that of the vassal. "Switzerland," says Sismondi, "which in so many respects resembles Scotland – in its lakes, its mountains, its climate and the character, manners and habits of its children – was likewise at the same period parcelled out among a small number of lords. If the Counts of Kyburgh, of Lentzburg, of Hapsburg and of Gruyeres, had been protected by the English laws, they would find themselves at the present day precisely

17

in the condition in which the Earls of Sutherland were twenty years ago. Some of them would perhaps have had the same taste for *improvements,* and several republics would have been expelled from the Alps, to make room for flocks of sheep. But while the law has given to the Swiss peasant a guarantee of perpetuity, it is to the Scottish laird that it has extended this guarantee in the British Empire, leaving the peasant in a precarious situation. The clan – recognized at first by the captain, whom they followed in war, and obeyed for their common advantage, as his friends and relations, then as his soldiers, then as his vassals, then as his farmers – he has come finally to regard as hired labourers, whom he may perchance allow to remain on the soil of their common country for his own advantage, but whom he has the power to expel so soon as he no longer finds it for his interest to keep them."

'Arguments like those of Sismondi, however much their force may be felt on the Continent, would be formidable at home in only a time of revolution, when the very foundations of society would be unfixed, and opinions set loose, to pull down or re-construct at pleasure. But it is surely interesting to note how, in the course of events, that very law of England which, in the view of the Frenchman, has done the Highland peasant so much less and the Highland chief so much more than justice, is bidding fair, in the case of Sutherland at least, to carry its rude equalizing remedy along with it. Between the years 1811 and 1820, fifteen thousand inhabitants of this northern district were ejected from their snug inland farms, by means for which we would in vain seek a precedent, except, perchance, in the history of the Irish massacre.

'But though the interior of the county was thus improved into a desert, in which there are many thousands of sheep but few human habitations, let it not be supposed by the reader that its general population was in any degree lessened. So far was this from being the case that the census of 1821 showed an increase over the census of 1811 of more than two hundred and the present population of Sutherland exceeds by a thousand its population before the change. The county has not been depopulated – its population has been merely arranged after a new fashion. The late Duchess found it spread equally over the interior and the sea-coast, and in very comfortable circumstances – she left it compressed into a wretched selvage of poverty and suffering that fringes the county on its eastern and western shores, and the law which enabled her to make such an arrangement, in spite of the ancient rights of the poor Highlander, is now about to step in to make her family pay the penalty. The southern kingdom must and will give us a poor-law; and then shall the selvage of deep poverty which fringes the sea-coasts of Sutherland avenge on the titled proprietor of the county both his mother's error and his own. If our British laws, unlike those of Switzerland, failed miserably in her day in protecting the vassal, they will more than fail in those of her successor in protecting the lord. Our political economists shall have an opportunity of reducing their arguments regarding the improvements in Sutherland into a few arithmetical terms, which the merest tyro will be able to grapple with.

'It is poor comfort when one sees a country ruined to know that the perpetrators of the mischief have not ruined it to their own advantage. I intend to show how remarkable in the case of Sutherland this ruin has been, and how very extreme the infatuation which continues to possess its hereditary lord. I am old enough to remember the county in its original state, when it was at once the happiest and one of the most exemplary districts in Scotland, and passed a considerable time among its hills; I know it now, with its melancholy and dejected people that wear out life in their comfortless cottages on the seashore. The problem solved in this remote district of the kingdom deserves the attention which it seems to be just beginning to draw, both from Great Britain and from Europe.

'But what, asks the reader, was the condition with regard to circumstances and means of living of these Sutherland Highlanders? Answers vary, depending on the class selected from among them as specimens of the whole, the honesty of the party who replies and his acquaintance with the circumstances of the poorer people of Scotland generally. The county had poorer localities, in which, for a month or two in the summer season, when the stock of grain from the previous year was running out and the crops on the ground had not yet ripened for use, the people experienced a considerable degree of scarcity – such scarcity as a mechanic in the South feels when he has been a fortnight out of employment. But the Highlander had resources in these seasons which the mechanic has not. He had his cattle and his wild herbs. It has been stated by the advocates of the change which has ruined Sutherland, as proof of the extreme hardship of the Highlander's condition, that at such times he might have eaten broth made of nettles mixed up with a little oatmeal or have had recourse to the expedient of bleeding his cattle and making the blood into a sort of pudding. And it is quite true that the Sutherlandshire Highlander was in the habit at such times of having recourse to such food. It is equally true, however, that the statement is just as little conclusive regarding his condition as if it were alleged that there must always be famine in France when the people eat the hind legs of frogs, or in Italy when they make dishes of snails. With regard to the general comfort of the people in their old condition, there are better tests than can be drawn from the kind of food they occasionally ate. The country hears often of dearth in Sutherland now. Every year in which the crop falls a little below average in other districts is a year of famine there but the country never heard of dearth in Sutherland then. There were very few among the holders of its small inland farms who had not saved a little money. Their circumstances were such that their moral nature found full room to develop itself, and in a way the world has rarely witnessed. Never was there a happier or more contented people or a people more strongly attached to the soil, and not one of them now lives in the altered circumstances on which they were so rudely precipitated by the landlord, who does not look back on this period of comfort and enjoyment with sad and hopeless regret.

'But we have not yet said how this ruinous revolution was effected in Sutherland – how the aggravations of the *mode*, if we may so speak, still fester in the recollections of the people – or how thoroughly that policy of the lord of the soil, through which he now seems determined to complete the work of ruin which his predecessor began, harmonizes with its worst details. We must first relate a disastrous change which took place in the noble family of Sutherland and which, though it dates fully eighty years back, may be regarded as pregnant with the disasters which afterwards befell the county.

'The marriage of the young countess into a noble English family was fraught with further disaster to the county. There are many Englishmen intelligent enough to tell the difference between a smoky cottage of turf and a whitewashed cottage of stone, whose judgments on their respective inhabitants would be of little value. Sutherland, as a county of men, stood higher at this period than perhaps any other district in the British Empire but it by no means stood high as a county of farms and cottages. The marriage of the countess brought a new set of eyes upon it, eyes accustomed to quite a different face of things. It seemed a wild, rude county where all was wrong and all had to be set right – a sort of Russia on a small scale, that had just got another Peter the Great to civilize it, or a sort of barbarous Egypt, with an energetic Ali Pasha at its head. Even the vast wealth and great liberality of the Stafford family militated against this hapless county! It enabled them to treat it as a mere subject of an interesting experiment, in which gain to themselves was really no object – nearly as little as if they had resolved on dissecting a dog alive for the benefit of science. It was a still further disadvantage that they had to carry on their experiment by the hands, and to watch its first effects with the eyes, of others. The agonies of the dog might have had their softening influence on a dissector who held the knife himself but there could be no such influence exerted over him if he merely issued orders to his footman that the dissection should be completed, remaining himself out of sight and out of hearing. The plan of improvement sketched out by this English family was exceedingly easy of conception. Here is a vast tract of land, furnished with two distinct sources of wealth. Its shores may be made the seats of extensive fisheries and the whole of its interior parcelled out into productive sheep farms. All is waste in its present state; it has no fisheries and two-thirds of its internal produce is consumed by the inhabitants. It had contributed, for the use of the community and the landlord, its large herds of black cattle, but the English family saw that, for every pound of beef which it produced, it could be made to produce two pounds of mutton, and perhaps a pound of fish in addition. It was resolved, therefore, that the inhabitants of the central districts, as they were mere Celts and allegedly could not be transformed into store farmers, should be marched down to the seaside, there to convert themselves into fishermen, on the shortest possible notice. A few farmers of capital, of the industrious Lowland race, should be invited to occupy the new sub-divisions of the interior.

'And, pray, what objections can be urged against so liberal and large-minded a scheme? The poor inhabitants of the interior had very serious objections to urge against it. Their humble dwellings were of their own making; they themselves had broken in their little fields from the waste; from time immemorial, far beyond the reaches of history, had they possessed their mountain holdings – they had defended them so well of old that the soil was still virgin ground, in which the invader had found only a grave. Their young men were now in foreign lands, fighting at the command of their chieftainess the battles of their country, in the character not of hired soldiers but of men who saw these very holdings as their stake in the quarrel. To them, the scheme seemed fraught with the most flagrant injustice. Were it to be suggested by some Chartist convention in a time of revolution that Sutherland might be still further improved – that it was really a piece of great waste to let the revenues of so extensive a district be squandered by one individual, that it would be better to appropriate them to the use of the community in general, that the community in general might be still further benefited by the removal of the said individual from Dunrobin to a roadside, where he might be profitably employed in breaking stones – and that this new arrangement could not be entered on too soon, the noble Duke would not be any more astonished or rendered any more indignant by the scheme than were the Highlanders of Sutherland by the scheme of his predecessor.

'The reader must bear in mind that, if atrocities unexampled in Britain for at least a century were perpetrated in the clearing of Sutherland, there was a species of at least passive resistance on the part of the people, which in some degree provoked them. Had the Highlanders, on receiving orders, marched down to the sea-coast and become fishermen with the readiness with which a regiment deploys on review day, the atrocities would, we doubt not, have been much fewer. But though the orders were very distinct, the Highlanders were very unwilling to obey and the severities formed merely a part of the means through which the necessary obedience was ultimately secured. A single case illustrates the process.

'In March, 1814, a large proportion of the Highlanders of Farr and Kildonan, two parishes in Sutherland, were summoned to quit their farms in the following May. In a few days after, the surrounding heath on which they pastured their cattle and from which, at that season, the sole supply of herbage is derived (for in those northern districts the grass springs late, and the cattle fodder in the spring months depends chiefly on the heather) were set on fire and burned up. It was the kind of policy which men consider allowable in a state of war. The starving cattle went roaming over the burned pastures and found nothing to eat. Many of them died, and most of the remainder, though in miserable condition, the Highlanders were forced to sell. Most of the able-bodied men were engaged in this latter business some way from home when the dreaded term-day arrived. The pasturage had been destroyed before the term, although legally it was still the property of the poor Highlanders, but term-day was allowed to pass before they were disturbed in their homes.

Then the work of demolition began. A large party of men with a factor at their head entered the district and began pulling down the houses over the heads of the inhabitants. In an extensive tract of country, not a human dwelling was left standing and then, to prevent their temporary re-erection, the destroyers set fire to the wrecks. In one day the people were deprived of home and shelter and left exposed to the elements. Many deaths are said to have ensued from alarm, fatigue and cold.'

Mr. Hugh Miller then corroborates in detail the atrocities, cruelties and personal hardships described by Donald MacLeod and proceeds: 'But to employ the language of Southey,

> "Things such as these, we know, must be
> At every famous victory."

'And in this instance the victory of the lord of the soil over the children of the soil was signal and complete. In little more than nine years a population of fifteen thousand individuals were removed from the interior of Sutherland to its sea-coasts or had emigrated to America. The inland districts were converted into deserts through which the traveller may take a long day's journey, amid ruins that still bear the scars of fire, and grassy patches betraying, when the evening sun casts aslant its long deep shadows, the half-effaced lines of the plough.'

After pointing out how at the Disruption sites for churches were refused, Miller proceeds:

'We have exhibited to our readers, in the *clearing* of Sutherland, a process of ruin so thoroughly disastrous that it might be deemed scarcely possible to render it more complete. And yet with all its apparent completeness, it admitted of a supplementary process. To employ one of the striking figures of Scripture, it was possible to grind into powder what had been previously broken into fragments – to degrade the poor inhabitants to a still lower level than that on which they had been so cruelly precipitated – though persons of a not very original cast of mind might have found it difficult to say how the Duke of Sutherland has been ingenious enough to fall on exactly the one proper expedient for supplementing their ruin. All in mere circumstance and situation that could lower and deteriorate had been present as ingredients in the first process; but there still remained for the people, however reduced to poverty or broken in spirit, the consolations of religion. Sabbath-days came round with their humanizing influences and, under the teachings of the gospel, the poor and the oppressed looked longingly forward to a future scene of being in which there is no poverty or oppression. They still possessed, amid their misery, something positively good, of which it was impossible to deprive them, and hence the ability derived to the present lord of Sutherland of deepening and rendering more signal the ruin accomplished by his predecessor.

'This harmonizes only too well with the mode in which the interior of Sutherland was cleared and the improved cottages of its sea-coasts erected. The plan has two items. No sites are to be granted in the district for Free Churches and no dwelling-houses for Free Church ministers. The climate is severe, the winters prolonged and stormy, the roads which connect the chief seats of population with the neighbouring counties dreary and long. Might not ministers and people be eventually worn out in this way? Such is the part of the plan which his Grace and his Grace's creatures can afford to present to the light. But there are supplementary items of a somewhat darker kind. The poor cottars are, in the great majority of cases, tenants-at-will; and great trouble has been taken to inform them that, to the crime of entertaining and sheltering a Protesting minister, the penalty of ejection from their holdings must inevitably attach. The laws of Charles have again returned in this unhappy district, and free and tolerating Scotland has got, in the nineteenth century, as in the seventeenth, its intercommuned ministers. We shall not say that the intimation has emanated from the Duke. It is the misfortune of such men that there creep around them creatures whose business it is to anticipate their wishes but who, at times, doubtless, instead of anticipating misinterpret them, and who, even when not very much mistaken, impart to whatever they do the mark of their own low and menial natures and thus exaggerate in the act the intention of their masters. We do not say, therefore, that the intimation has emanated from the Duke, but that an exemplary Sutherlandshire minister of the Protesting Church, who resigned his worldly all for the sake of his principles, had recently to travel, in order to preach to his flock, a long journey of forty-four miles outwards, and as much in return, and all this without taking shelter under any roof or partaking of any refreshment other than the small store of provisions which he had carried with him from his new home. Willingly would the poor Highlanders have received him at any risk but, knowing from experience what a

Sutherlandshire removal means, he preferred enduring any amount of hardship rather than that the hospitality of his people should be made the cause of their ruin.

'A lady of Sutherland was threatened with ejection from her home because she had offered shelter to one of the Protesting clergy, an aged and venerable man who had quitted the neighbouring manse, his home for many years, because he could no longer enjoy it in consistency with his principles. That aged and venerable man was the lady's own father. What amount of oppression of a smaller and more petty character may not be expected in the circumstances when cases such as these are found to stand but a very little over the ordinary level?

'In the parish of Dornoch, where his Grace is fortunately not the sole landowner, there has been a site procured on the most generous terms from Sir George Gunn Munro of Pontyzfield. This gentleman, believing himself to own a hereditary right to a quarry, which, though on the Duke's ground, had been long used by the proprietors of the district generally, instructed the builder to take from it the stones which he needed. Never had the quarry been prohibited before, but on this occasion a stringent interdict arrested its use. If his Grace could not prevent a hated Free Church from arising in the district, he could at least add to the expense of its erection. We have even heard that the portion of the building previously erected had to be pulled down and the stones returned.

'How are we to account for a hostility so determined, and so base? In two different ways, and in both the people of Scotland have a direct interest. If his Grace entertained a very intense regard for Established Presbytery, then he himself would probably be a Presbyterian of the Establishment. But such is not the case. The church into which he would force the people has been long since deserted by him. The secret of the course which he pursues can have no connection with religious motive or belief. Let us remark, rather in the way of embodying a fact than imputing a motive, that with his present views and in his present circumstances, it may not seem particularly his Grace's interests to make the county of Sutherland a happy or desirable home to the people of Scotland. It may not be his Grace's interests that the population of the district should increase. The clearing of the sea-coast may seem as beneficial to his Grace's welfare now as the clearing of the interior was in the interests of his predecessor thirty years ago; nay, it is quite possible that his Grace may be led to regard the clearing of the coast as the better and more important clearing of the two. Let it not be forgotten that a poor-law hangs over Scotland – that the shores of Sutherland are covered with what seems one vast straggling village, inhabited by an impoverished and ruined people – and that the coming assessment may fall so heavily that the extra profits accruing to his Grace from his large sheep farms may go only a small way towards supporting his extra paupers. It is quite likely that he may live to find the revolution effected by his predecessor taking to itself the form, not of a crime – for that would be nothing – but of a disastrous and very terrible blunder.

'There is another remark which may prove worth the consideration of the reader. Ever since the completion of the fatal experiment which ruined Sutherland, the noble family through which it was originated and carried on have shown great fear of having its real results made public. Volumes of special pleading have been written on the subject – pamphlets have been published, laboured articles have been inserted in widely-spread reviews, statistical accounts have been watched over with the most careful surveillance. If the misrepresentations of the press could have altered the facts, famine would not be gnawing the vitals of Sutherland in a year a little less abundant than its predecessors, nor would the dejected and oppressed people be feeding their discontent, amid present misery, with memories of a happier past. If a singularly well-conditioned and wholesome district of country has been converted into one wide ulcer of wretchedness, it must be confessed that the sore has been carefully bandaged up from the public eye. If there has been little done for its cure, there has at least been much done for its concealment.

'Now, let it be remembered that a Free Church threatened to insert a *tent* into this wound and so keep it open. It has been said that the Gaelic language removes a district further from the influence of

English opinion than an ocean of three thousand miles, and that the British public know better what is doing in New York than what is doing in Lewis or Skye. And hence one cause, at least, of the thick obscurity that has so long enveloped the miseries which the poor Highlander has had to endure and the oppressions to which he has been subjected. The Free Church threatens to translate her wrongs into English and to give them currency in the general mart of opinion. She might possibly be no silent spectator of conflagrations such as those which characterized the first general improvement of Sutherland, nor yet of such Egyptian schemes of house-building as that which formed part of the improvements of a later plan. She might betray the real state of the district and thus render laborious misrepresentation pointless. She might effect a diversion in favour of the people and shake the foundations of the hitherto despotic power which has so long weighed them down. She might do for Sutherland what Cobbett promised to do but had not character enough to accomplish, and what he did not live even to attempt. A combination of circumstances have conspired to vest in a Scottish proprietor, in this northern district, a more despotic power than even the most absolute monarchs of the Continent possess. It is no great wonder that that proprietor should be jealous of the introduction of an element which threatens materially to lessen it. And so he struggles hard to exclude the Free Church and, though no member of the Establishment himself, declares warmly in its behalf. From the Establishment as now constituted he can have nothing to fear and the people nothing to hope.

'How might his Grace the Duke of Sutherland be most effectually met in this matter so that the case of toleration and freedom of conscience may be maintained in the extensive district which God has consigned to his stewardship? We are familiar with the Celtic character as developed in the Highlands of Scotland. Highlanders, up to a certain point, are the most docile, patient, enduring of men but, that point once passed, endurance ceases and the all too gentle lamb starts up an angry lion. The spirit is stirred and maddens at the sight of the naked weapon and, in its headlong rush upon the enemy, discipline can neither check nor control it. Let our oppressed Highlanders of Sutherland beware. They have suffered much but, so far as man is the agent, their battles can be fought only on the arena of public opinion, and on that ground which the political field may be soon found to furnish.

'Let us follow, for a little, the poor Highlanders of Sutherland to the sea-coast. It would be easy dwelling on the terrors of their expulsion and multiplying facts of horror but, had there been no subsequent permanent deterioration in their condition, these, all harrowing and repulsive as they were, would have mattered less. Sutherland would have soon recovered the burning up of a few hundred hamlets or the loss of a few bed-ridden old people, who would just as surely have died under cover, though perhaps a few months later, as when exposed to the elements in the open. Even if it had lost a thousand of its best men in the way in which it lost so many at the storming of New Orleans, the blank would have been completely filled up before now. The calamities of fire or of decimation even, however distressing in themselves, never yet ruined a country. No calamity ruins a country that leaves the surviving inhabitants to develop, in their old circumstances, their old character and resources.

'In one of the eastern eclogues of Collins, where two shepherds are described as flying for their lives before the troops of a ruthless invader, we see with how much of the terrible the imagination of a poet could invest in the evils of war, when aggravated by pitiless barbarity. Fertile as that imagination was, there might be found new circumstances to heighten the horrors of the scene – circumstances beyond the reach of invention – in the retreat of the Sutherland Highlanders from the smoking ruins of their cottages to their allotments on the coast. We have heard of one man named Mackay, whose family at the time of the greater conflagration referred to by Macleod were all lying ill of fever, who had to carry two of his sick children on his back a distance of twenty-five miles. We have heard of the famished people blackening the shores like the crew of some vessel wrecked on an inhospitable coast, trying to sustain life by the shellfish and seaweed laid bare by the ebb. Many of their allotments, espe-

29

cially on the western coast, were barren in the extreme, unsheltered by bush or tree, and exposed to the sweeping sea winds, and in storms, to the blighting spray. It was found a matter of the extremest difficulty to keep the few cattle which they had retained from wandering, especially at night, into the better sheltered and more fertile interior. The poor animals were intelligent enough to read a practical comment on the nature of the change effected and, from the harshness of the shepherds to whom the care of the interior had been entrusted, they served materially to add to the distress of their unhappy masters. They were getting continually impounded and fines, in the form of trespass-money, were extracted from the already impoverished Highlanders. Many who had no money to give were obliged to pay by depositing some of their few portable articles of value, such as bed or body clothes or, more distressing still, watches, rings and pins – the only relics, in many instances, of brave men whose bones were mouldering under the fatal rampart at New Orleans or in the arid sands of Egypt, where the invincibles of Napoleon went down before the Highland bayonet. Their first efforts as fishermen were what might be expected from a rural people unaccustomed to the sea. The shores of Sutherland, for immense tracts together, are ironbound, and much exposed – open on the Eastern coast to the waves of the German Ocean and on the North and West to the long roll of the Atlantic. There could not be more perilous seas for the unpractised boatman to take his first lessons on but, though the casualties were numerous and the loss of life great, many of the younger Highlanders became expert fishermen. The experiment was harsh in the extreme but, so far, at least, it succeeded. It lies open, however, to other objections than those which have been urged against it on the score of its inhumanity.'

Mr. James Loch on the Sutherland Improvements

No country of Europe at any period of its history ever presented more formidable obstacles to the improvement of a people arising out of the prejudices and feelings of the people themselves. To the tacksman, it is clear from what has already been stated such a change could not be agreeable. Its effect was to alter his condition and remove him from a state of idle independence, in habits almost of equality with his chief, to a situation in which, although leading to real independence and wealth such as he never could arrive at in his original condition, his livelihood was to be obtained by his own physical efforts. Frequently this involved an application to pursuits which, although fully if not more respectable, were by him considered beneath the occupation of a gentleman. Nor could it be agreeable to him to lose that command and influence which he had previously exercised without control over his sub-tenants and dependants. It was at variance with every feeling and prejudice in which he had been brought up and educated. It required minds of no ordinary cast to rise above these feelings and men of unusual understanding and intellect were required to shake off habits so opposed to active industry and exertion. From a certain set of this class a real and determined opposition to any change was to be looked for. This expectation has not been disappointed and it is from individuals of this class, and persons connected with them, that those false and malignant representations have proceeded which have been so loudly and extensively circulated. Actuated by motives of a mere personal nature, regardless of the happiness of the people, whose improvement it was the great object of the landlord to effect, they attempted to make an appeal in favour of a set of people who were never before the objects of their commiseration, in order that they might, if possible, reduce them, for their own selfish purposes, to that state of degradation from which they had been just emancipated. This was by no means true of the majority of this class of gentlemen for the bulk of the most active improvers of Sutherland are natives, who, both as sheep farmers and as skilful and enterprising agriculturists, are equal to any in the kingdom. They have, with an intelligence and liberality of feeling which does them credit, embraced eagerly the new life of active exertion offered to them, seconding the views of the landlords with the utmost zeal, foresight and prudence. Out of the twenty-nine principal

31

tacksmen on the estate, seventeen are natives of Sutherland, four are Northumbrians, two are from the county of Moray, two from Roxburghshire, two from Caithness, one from Midlothian, and one from the Merse.

So strong, however, were the prejudices of the people that, even to those who were subjected to the power and control of the tacksman, this mode of life had charms which attached them strongly to it. He extended, in some degree, to the more respectable of those who were placed under him the same familiarity which he received from the chief. The burden of the outdoor work was cast upon the females. The men deemed such an occupation unworthy of them, continued labour of any sort being against their nature. They were contented with the most simple and the poorest fare. Like all mountaineers, accustomed to a life of irregular exertion with intervals of sloth, they were attached with a degree of enthusiasm only felt by the natives of a poor country to their own glen and mountainside, sticking firmly to the habits and homes of their fathers. No comfort was worth having if it was to be bought at the price of regular labour; no improvement worthy of adoption if it was to be obtained at the expense of the customs or the homes of their ancestors. So strongly did these feelings operate that it cost them nearly the same effort to remove from the spot in which they were born and brought up, though their new home was situated on the seashore at the mouth of their native strath or even in a neighbouring glen, as it cost them to make an exertion equal to transporting themselves across the Atlantic.

The cattle which they reared on the mountains, and from the sale of which they depended for the payment of their rents, were of the poorest description. During summer they procured a scanty sustenance, with much toil and labour, by roaming over the mountains while in winter they died in numbers for the want of support. In addition to this it had become universal practice to kill every second calf, on account of the want of winter keep. In the spring of 1807, there died in the parish of Kildonan alone two hundred cows, five hundred head of cattle and more than two hundred small horses.

As soon as the works, undertaken under the direction of the Par-

liamentary Commissioners, opened a prospect of removing the obstacles which stood in the way of the improvements of the people,
steps were taken to remodel and arrange these extensive properties.
The utmost caution and deliberation was used in doing so, and plans
were never more carefully considered, nor executed with more anxiety and tenderness. To aid the further arrangement of these matters,
application was made to William Young, Esq., of Inverurie, in the
county of Elgin, whose intelligence and energy had been demonstrated in what he had done upon his own estate. This gentleman
superintended the start of those vast improvements which were undertaken on the estate of Sutherland. The success of the measures
carried out under his direction, combined with the difficulties he
had to contend with, are the best proof of the ability and untiring
zeal with which he executed his duties, performed both to his own
credit and to the advantage of the country. The speed of the earlier
improvements was primarily the impulse and action inspired by his
intelligent and enterprising mind. Mr. Young resigned his superintendence in 1816, when the local management of the estate of Sutherland was entrusted to the present factor, Mr. Francis Suther, whose
good temper and judicious conduct in the immediate management
at Trentham recommended him to the situation he now holds. These
expectations have been fully justified by the manner in which he has
executed the details of the late arrangements, in which he was ably
assisted by Captain John Mackay, late of the 26th Foot, the factor of
Strathnaver, and Lieutenant George Gunn of the Royal Marines, Chief
of the Clan Gunn, factor of Assynt.

These gentlemen deserve equal credit for the manner in which
they have enforced and promoted the plans which were laid down
for the extension of the fisheries and the cultivation of the coast side,
as for their kind and careful conduct towards the people. Mr. Suther's
exertions in promoting and carrying into effect every arrangement
which was made for the encouragement and the success of the fishing station and village of Helmsdale require particular commenda-
tion.

It is well known that the borders of the two kingdoms were inhabited by a large population who, in their pursuits, manners and general structure of society, bore a considerable resemblance to that which existed in the Highlands of Scotland. When the union of the crowns, and those subsequent transactions which arose out of that event, rendered the maintenance of that irregular population not only unnecessary but a burden to the proprietor to whom the land belonged, the people were removed and the mountains were covered with sheep. It had been proved by the experience of the stock farmers of those mountain tracts, which comprise the northern districts of England and the southern parts of Scotland, that such situations were peculiarly suited for the maintenance of this species of stock. Taking this example as their guide, experience had still further proved that the central and western Highlands of Scotland were equally well calculated for the same end.

Reasoning from this success and observing that the climate of Sutherland, close to the ocean and considerably intersected by arms of the sea, was much more moderate than this latter district, it was fairly concluded that this county was even better suited to this system of management than the heights of Perthshire and Invernessshire. The inferior elevation of its mountains contributed still further to this effect and held out every encouragement to adopt the same course which had been pursued with such success in both parts of the kingdom.

The succession of those Alpine plants, which are common to the Cheviot Hills, when they are put under sheep, being also the natural herbage of the mountains of Sutherland, renders them still more suitable to this mode of occupation.

On the first melting of the snow, the cotton grass is found to have been growing rapidly; it forms a healthy and abundant food for sheep until about the beginning of May, at which time it is in seed. When, after a short interval, the deer hair takes its place, starting up almost instantaneously, and forming, in the course of one week (if the ground has been recently burned, and the weather be favourable) a green cover to the mountains. This plant grows with several varieties of bents until the end of July, when the cotton grass again begins to spring and, with the pry moss, comes a second time into flower in September, after which the heather and more heating plants continue until the frosts of winter. There is no part of these mountains over which the sheep cannot roam with ease in search of food, making the whole area available and profitable.

As there was every reason for concluding that the mountainous parts of the estate, and indeed of Sutherland, were as suitable for the maintenance of stock as they were unfit for the habitation of man, there could be no doubt as to the propriety of converting them into sheep walks, *provided* the people could be at the same time settled in situations where, by honest labour, they could obtain a decent livelihood and should not be exposed to the recurrence of those privations which so frequently afflicted them when living in the mountains. The local peculiarities of the county presented none of those advantages in disposing of and absorbing the surplus population which the borders of the two kingdoms and the southern and eastern Highlands had enjoyed. Besides, it had made no approximation to the state in which the rest of Scotland was placed when those changes were carried into effect. It had stood still in the midst of that career of improvement which had so splendidly distinguished the rest of the kingdom, and remained separated by its habits, prejudices and language from all around.

It had long been known that the coast of Sutherland abounded with many different kinds of fish, not only sufficient for the consumption of the country but enough to supply *to any extent* markets at home or abroad, when cured and salted. Besides the regular, abundant and continual supply of white fish on these shores, Sutherland is annually visited by one of those vast shoals of herrings which frequent the coast of Scotland. It seemed natural that the system for this remote district, in order that it might bear its responsibility in contributing its share to the general stock of the country, was to convert the mountainous districts into sheep walks, and to remove the inhabitants to the coast or to the valleys near the sea.

It will be seen that the object to be obtained by this arrangement was two-fold. It was, in the first place, to render this mountainous district contributory, as far as possible, to the general wealth and industry of the country and in the manner most suitable to its situation and peculiar circumstances. This was to be effected by making it produce a large supply of wool for the staple manufactory of England. The district was also to support as numerous, and a far more laborious and useful population than before. This required the conversion of the inhabitants of those districts to the habits of regular and continued industry, to enable them to bring to market a considerable surplus quantity of provisions, to supply the large towns in the south of the island or for export.

A policy well calculated to raise the importance and increase the happiness of the people who were the objects of the change, to benefit those to whom these extensive but hitherto unproductive possessions belonged and to promote the general prosperity of the nation – such was the system which was adopted. In carrying it into effect, every care was taken to explain the object proposed to be accomplished to those who were to be removed and to point out to them the ultimate advantages that would accrue to them.

This information was conveyed to the people by the factor personally or by written statements communicated by the ground officers. That nothing might be omitted in this respect, the different ministers and the principal tacksmen connected with the districts which were to be newly arranged, were written to, explaining fully and explicitly the intentions of the proprietors in adopting them. These gentlemen were particularly requested to impress upon the minds of the people the importance of agreeing to them, and to explain that the motives which dictated this step arose out of a real regard for their interests as well as for the general improvement of the estate.

It was admitted that it was not to be expected that the people should be immediately reconciled to the changes. But it was argued that, if this was so fully felt and so clearly admitted, the landlords must have been strongly convinced of the need to adopt the measures as leading to the happiness of those placed under their protection. These arguments had the desired effect and nothing can be more praiseworthy than the conduct of the people on quitting their original habitations for, although they left them with much regret, they did so in the most quiet, orderly and peaceable manner.

If, upon one occasion, in the earlier years of these arrangements, a momentary resistance was shown, it arose entirely from the misconduct of persons whose duty it was to have recommended and enforced obedience to the laws, instead of infusing feelings of a contrary description into the minds of the people. As soon as the interference of these persons was withdrawn, the poor people returned to their usual state of quietness and repose. All the statements giving a different account of their conduct are absolutely false, and a libel upon their good conduct.

These arrangements began in 1807, and have been carried on from that period as the different tacks expired, and afforded an opportunity of doing so. Bad years and the failure of crops continued to produce the same miserable effects they had always brought to that portion of the population which still lived among the mountains. The years 1812–13 and 1816–17 were particularly severe.

During the latter period the people suffered extremes of want and of human misery, in spite every assistance given to them through the bounty of their landlords. Their wretchedness was so great that, after pawning everything they owned to the fishermen on the coast, those who had no cattle were forced to come down from the hills and gather cockles on the shore. Those who lived in the more remote situations of the country were obliged to subsist upon broth made of nettles, thickened with a little oatmeal. Those who had cattle had recourse to the still more wretched expedient of bleeding them and mixing the blood with oatmeal, which they afterwards cut into slices and fried. Those who had a little money came down and slept all night upon the beach, to watch the boats returning from fishing, hoping to obtain some of the catch.

In order to alleviate this misery, every exertion was made by Lord Stafford. To those who had cattle he advanced money to the amount of above three thousand pounds.

To supply those who had no cattle, he sent meal into the country to the amount of nearly nine thousand pounds. In addition to this,

Lady Stafford distributed money to each parish on the estate. In order that no effort should be wasted, it was arranged that I, as the head of his Lordship's affairs, should go to Dunrobin to arrange with the local management and the clergymen the best and most effective way of distributing his Lordship's relief. While such was the distress of those who still remained among the hills, *it was hardly felt by those who had been settled upon the coast*. Their new occupation as fishermen made them not only independent of that which produced the misery of their neighbours but enabled them at the same time, in some degree, to contribute towards their support, both by the fish they were able to sell to them, and also by the regular payment of their rents. It need hardly be stated that the wretched sufferers not only required to be relieved but failed entirely in the payment of what they owed the landlord.

Mrs. Harriet Beecher Stowe on the Sutherland Clearances

As to those ridiculous stories about the Duchess of Sutherland which have found their way into many of the prints in America, one has only to be here, moving in society, to see how excessively absurd they are.

All my way through Scotland and England, I was associating from day to day with people of every religious denomination and every rank of life. I have been with dissenters and with churchmen; with the national Presbyterian Church and the free Presbyterian, with Quakers and Baptists.

In all these circles I have heard the great and noble of the land freely spoken of and canvassed and, if there had been the least shadow of a foundation for any such accusations, I certainly should have heard it recognized in some manner. If in no other, such warm friends as I have heard speak would have alluded to the subject in the way of defence, but I have actually never heard any allusion of any sort, as if there was anything to be explained or accounted for.

As I have said before, the Howard family, to which the duchess belongs, is one which has always been on the side of popular rights and popular reform. Lord Carlisle, her brother, has been a leader of the people, particularly during the time of the corn-law reformation, and *she* has been known to take a wide and generous interest in all these subjects. Everywhere that I have moved through Scotland and England, I have heard her kindness of heart, her affability of manner, and her attention to the feelings of others spoken of as marked characteristics.

Imagine, then, what people must think when they find in respectable American prints the absurd story of her turning her tenants out into the snow and ordering the cottages to be set on fire over their heads because they would not go out.

But, if you ask how such an absurd story could ever have been made up, I answer that it is the exaggerated report of a movement made by the present Duke of Sutherland's father in the year 1811, which was part of a great movement that passed through the Highlands of Scotland when the advancing progress of civilization began to make it necessary to change the estates from military to agricultural establishments.

Soon after the union of the crowns of England and Scotland, the border chiefs found it profitable to adopt upon their estates that system of agriculture to which their hills were adapted, rather than to continue the maintenance of military retainers. Instead of keeping garrisons with small armies in a district, they decided to keep only so many as could profitably cultivate the land. The effect of this, of course, was like disbanding an army. It threw many people out of employ and forced them to seek a home elsewhere. Like many other movements which, in their final results, are beneficial to society, this was at first vehemently resisted and had to be carried into effect in some cases by force. As I have said, it began first in the southern counties of Scotland, soon after the union of the English and Scottish crowns, and gradually crept northward, one county after another yielding to the change. To a certain extent, as it progressed northward, the demand for labour in the great towns absorbed the surplus population but, when it came into the extreme Highlands, this refuge was wanting. Emigration to America now became the resource and the surplus population were induced to this by means such as the Colonization Society now recommends and approves for promoting emigration to Liberia.

The first farm so formed on the Sutherland estate was in 1806. The great change was made in 1811–12 and completed in 1819–20.

The Sutherland estates are in the most northern portion of Scotland. The distance of this district from the more advanced parts of the kingdom, the total want of roads, the unfrequent communication by sea, and the want of towns, made it necessary to adopt a different course in regard to the location of the Sutherland population from that which circumstances had provided in other parts of Scotland, where they had been removed from the bleak and uncultivable mountains. They had lots given them near the sea, or in more fertile spots, where, by labour and industry, they might maintain themselves. They had two years allowed them for preparing for the change, without payment of rent. Timber for their houses was given, and many other facilities for assisting their change.

The general agent of the Sutherland estate is Mr. Loch. In a speech by this gentleman in the House of Commons on the second reading of the Scotch Poor-Law Bill, 12th June, 1845, he states the following fact with regard to the management of the Sutherland estate during this period, from 1811 to 1833, which certainly can speak for itself: 'I can state as from fact that, from 1811 to 1833, not one sixpence of rent has been received from that county but, on the contrary, there has been sent there, for the benefit and improvement of the people, a sum exceeding sixty thousand pounds.'

Mr. Loch goes on in the same speech to say, 'There is no set of people more industrious than the people of Sutherland. Thirty years ago they were engaged in illegal distillation to a very great extent; at the present moment there is not, I believe, an illegal still in the county. Their morals have improved as those habits have been abandoned and they have added many hundreds, I believe thousands, of acres to the land in cultivation since they were placed upon the shore.

'Before the change to which I have referred, they exported very few cattle, and hardly anything else. They were also, every now and then, exposed to all the difficulties of extreme famine. In the years 1812–13 and 1816–17, so great was the misery that it was necessary to send down oatmeal for their supply to the amount of nine thousand pounds and that was given to the people. But, since industrious habits were introduced and they were settled within reach of fishing, no such calamity has overtaken them. Their condition was then so low that they were obliged to bleed their cattle during the winter and mix the blood with the remnant of meal they had, in order to save from them starvation.

'Since then the country has improved so much that, in 1815, the fish which they exported from one village alone, Helmsdale (which, previous to 1811, did not exist) amounted to five thousand, three hundred and eighteen barrels of herring. In 1844, there were thirty-seven thousand, five hundred and ninety-four barrels, giving employment to about three thousand, nine hundred people. This extends over the whole of the county, in which fifty-six thousand barrels were cured.

'Do not let me be supposed to say that there are not cases requiring attention – it must be so in a large population – but there can be no means taken by a landlord, or by those under him, that are not bestowed upon that tenantry.

'It has been said that the contribution by the heritor (the duke) to one kirk session for the poor was only six pounds. Now, in the eight parishes which are called Sutherland proper, the amount of the contribution of the Duke of Sutherland to the kirk session is forty-two pounds a year. That is a very small sum but that sum merely is so given because the landlord thinks that he can distribute his charity in a more beneficial manner to the people and the amount of charity which he gives – and which, I may say, is settled on them, for it is given regularly – is above four hundred and fifty pounds a year.

'Therefore the statements that have been made, so far from being correct, are in every way an exaggeration of what is the fact. No portion of the kingdom has advanced in prosperity so much and, if the honourable member (Mr. S. Crawford) will go down there, I will

41

give him every facility for seeing the state of the people, and he shall judge with his own eyes whether my representation be not correct. I could go through a great many other particulars but I will not trouble the House now with them. The statements I have made are accurate, and I am quite ready to prove them in any way that is necessary.'

The same Mr. Loch has published a pamphlet, in which he has traced out the effects of the system pursued on the Sutherland estate in many very important particulars. It appears from this that before 1811 the people were generally sub-tenants to middlemen, who exacted high rents and also various perquisites, such as the delivery of poultry and eggs, giving so many days' labour in harvest time, cutting and carrying peat and stones for building.

Since 1811, the people have become immediate tenants at a greatly diminished rate of rent and released from all these exactions. For instance, in two parishes, in 1812, the rents were one thousand five hundred and ninety-three pounds, and in 1823 they were only nine hundred and seventy-two pounds. In another parish the reduction of rents has amounted, on an average, to thirty-six per cent. Before 1811, the houses were turf huts of the poorest description, in many instances the cattle being kept under the same roof with the family. Since 1811, a large proportion of their houses have been rebuilt in a superior manner, the landlord having paid them for their old timber, where it could not be moved, and having also contributed the new timber with lime.

Before 1811, all the rents of the estates were used for the personal profit of the landlord but, since that time, both by the present duke and his father, all the rents have been expended on improvements in the county, besides sixty thousand pounds more which have been remitted from England for the purpose. This money has been spent on churches, schoolhouses, harbours, public inns, roads and bridges.

In 1811, there was not a carriage-road in the county, and only two bridges. Since that time four hundred and thirty miles of road have been constructed on the estate, at the expense of the proprietor and tenants. There is not a turnpike-gate in the county and yet the roads are kept perfect.

Before 1811, the mail was conveyed entirely by a foot runner, and there was only one post-office in the county. There was no direct post across the county, but letters to the north and west were forwarded once a month. A mail-coach has since been established, to which the late Duke of Sutherland contributed more than two thousand six hundred pounds; and since 1834 mail-gigs have been established to convey letters to the north and west coasts, towards which the Duke of Sutherland contributes three hundred pounds a year. There are sixteen post-offices and sub-offices in the county. Before 1811, there was no inn in the county fit for the reception of strangers. Since that time there have been fourteen inns either built or enlarged by the duke.

Before 1811, there was scarcely a cart on the estate; all the carriage was done on the backs of ponies. The cultivation of the interior was generally executed with a rude kind of spade, and there was not a gig in the county. In 1845, there were one thousand, one hundred and thirty carts owned on the estate, and seven hundred and eight ploughs, also forty-one gigs.

Before 1812, there was no baker and only two shops. In 1845, there were eight bakers and forty-six grocers' shops, in nearly all of which shoe-blacking was sold to some extent, an unmistakable evidence of advancing civilization.

In 1808, the cultivation of the coast side of Sutherland was so defective that it was necessary often, in a fall of snow, to cut down the young Scotch firs to feed the cattle on, and in 1808 hay had to be imported. *Now* the coast side of Sutherland exhibits an extensive district of land cultivated according to the best principles of modern agriculture; several thousand acres have been added to the arable land by these improvements.

Before 1811, there were no woodlands of any extent on the estate and timber had to be obtained from a distance. Since that time many thousand acres of woodland have been planted, the thinnings of which, being sold to the people at a moderate rate, have greatly increased their comfort and improved their domestic arrangements.

Before 1811, there were only two blacksmiths in the county. In

1845, there were forty-two blacksmiths and sixty-three carpenters. Before 1829, the exports of the county consisted of black cattle of an inferior description, pickled salmon and some ponies but these were precarious sources of profit, as many died in winter for want of food; for example, in the spring of 1807, two hundred cows, five hundred cattle and more than two hundred ponies died in the parish of Kildonan alone. Since that time the measures pursued by the Duke of Sutherland in introducing improved breeds of cattle and pigs and modes of agriculture have produced results in exports which tell their own story. About forty thousand sheep and one hundred and eighty thousand fleece of wool are exported annually; also fifty thousand barrels of herring.

The whole fishing village of Helmsdale has been built since that time. It now contains from thirteen to fifteen curing yards covered with slate and several streets with houses similarly built. The herring fishery, which has been mentioned as so productive, has been established since the change, and affords employment to three thousand nine hundred people.

Since 1811, also, a savings-bank has been established in every parish, of which the Duke of Sutherland is patron and treasurer, and the savings have been very considerable.

The education of the children of the people has been a subject of deep interest to the Duke of Sutherland. Besides the parochial schools (which answer, I suppose, to our district schools), of which the greater number have been rebuilt or repaired at an expense exceeding what is legally required for such purposes, the Duke of Sutherland contributes to the support of several schools for young females, at which sewing and other branches of education are taught. In 1844, he agreed to establish twelve General Assembly schools, in such parts of the county as were without the sphere of the parochial schools, and to build schools and schoolmasters' houses, which will, upon an average, cost two hundred pounds each; and to contribute annually two hundred pounds in aid of salaries to the teachers, besides a garden and cow's grass. In 1845, he made an arrangement with the education committee of the Free Church, whereby no child, of whatever persuasion, will be beyond the reach of moral and religious education.

There are five medical gentlemen on the estate, three of whom receive allowances from the Duke of Sutherland for attendance on the poor in the districts in which they reside.

A flourishing agricultural association, or farmers' club, has been formed under the patronage of the Duke of Sutherland, of which the other proprietors in the county and the larger tenantry are members. They have recently invited Professor Johnston to visit Sutherland and give lectures on agricultural chemistry.

The total population of the Sutherland estate is twenty-one thousand, seven hundred and eighty-four. To have the charge and care of so large an estate must require very systematic arrangements, but a talent for system seems to be rather the forte of the English.

The estate is first divided into three districts and each district is under the superintendence of a factor, who communicates with the duke through a general agent. Besides this, when the duke is on the estate, which is during a portion of every year, he receives on Monday whoever of his tenants wishes to see him. Their complaints or wishes are presented in writing; he takes them into consideration, and gives written replies.

Besides the three factors there is a ground officer, or sub-factor, in every parish, and an agriculturist in the Dunrobin district, who gives particular attention to instructing the people in the best methods of farming. The factors, the ground officers and the agriculturists, all work to one common end. They teach the advantages of draining; of ploughing deep and forming their ridges in straight lines; of constructing tanks for saving liquid manure. The young farmers also pick up a great deal of knowledge when working as ploughmen or labourers on the more immediate grounds of the estate.

The head agent, Mr. Loch, has been kind enough to put into my hands a general report of the condition of the estate, which he drew up for the inspection of the Duke, 12th May, 1853, and in which he goes minutely over the condition of every part of the estate.

One anecdote of the former Duke of Sutherland will show the spirit which has influenced the family in their management of the estate. In 1817, when there was much suffering on account of bad seasons, the Duke of Sutherland sent down his chief agent to look into the condition of the people, who asked the ministers of the parishes to send in their lists of poor. To his surprise, it was found that there were located on the estate four hundred and eight families, or two thousand persons, who had settled there without leave. Though they had no legal title to remain where they were, no hesitation was shown in supplying them with food in the same manner as those who were tenants, on the condition that on the first opportunity they should take cottages on the seashore, and become industrious people. It was the constant object of the Duke to keep the rents of his poorer tenants at a nominal amount.

What led me more particularly to enquire into these facts was that I received by mail, while in London, an account containing some of these stories which had been industriously circulated in America. There were dreadful accounts of cruelties practised in the process of inducing the tenants to change their places of residence.

Mr. Loch, the agent, says, 'I must notice the only thing like a fact stated in the newspaper extract which you sent to me, wherein Mr. Sellar is accused of acts of cruelty towards some of the people. This Mr. Sellar tested by bringing an action against the then Sheriff-substitute of the county. He obtained a verdict for heavy damages. The Sheriff, by whom the slander was propagated, left the county. Both are since dead.'

Having, through Lord Shaftesbury's kindness, received the benefit of Mr. Loch's corrections, I am permitted to make a little further extract from his reply. He says:

'In addition to what I was able to say in my former letter, I received from one of the most determined opposers of the measures, who travelled to the north of Scotland as editor of a newspaper, a letter regretting all he had written on the subject, being convinced that he was entirely misinformed. As you take so much interest in the subject, I will conclude by saying that nothing could exceed the prosperity of the county during the past year; their stock, sheep and other things sold at high prices; their crops of grain and turnips were never so good and the potatoes were free from all disease: rents have been paid better than was ever known.

As an instance of the improved habits of the farmers, no house is now built for them that they do not require a hot bath and water-closets.'

From this long epitome you can gather the following results. First, if the system were a bad one, the Duchess of Sutherland had nothing to do with it, since it was first introduced in 1806, the year Her Grace was born; and the accusation against Mr. Sellar dates in 1811, when Her Grace was five or six years old. The Sutherland arrangements were completed in 1819 and Her Grace was not married to the Duke till 1823, so that, had the arrangement been the worst in the world, it is nothing to the purpose so far as she is concerned.

As to whether the arrangement is a bad one, the facts which have been stated speak for themselves. To my view, it is an almost sublime instance of the benevolent employment of superior wealth and power in shortening the struggles of advancing civilization and elevating in a few years a whole community to a point of education and material prosperity, which, unassisted, they might never have obtained.

Reply to Mrs. Beecher Stowe by Mr. Donald Macleod

From 1812 to 1820, the whole interior of the county of Sutherland was in eight years converted to a solitary wilderness. The inhabitants of Sutherland were advancing rapidly in the science of agriculture and education and were, by nature and exemplary training, the bravest, the most moral and most patriotic people that ever existed (even admitting a few of them did violate the excise laws, the only sin which Mr. Loch and all the rest of their avowed enemies could bring against them). The voice of man praising God is not to be heard, nor the image of God upon man to be seen. You can set a compass with twenty miles of a radius upon it and go round with it full stretched and not find one acre of land within the circumference which has come under the plough for the last thirty years, except a few in the parishes of Lairg and Tongue, all under mute brute animals. This is the advancement of civilization, is it not, madam?

Return now with me to the beginning of your elaborate eulogy on the Duchess of Sutherland and, if you are open to conviction, I think you should be convinced that I never published nor circulated in the American, English or Scottish publications any ridiculous, absurd stories about Her Grace of Sutherland. An abridgement of my studies is now in the hands of the public and you may peruse them. I stand by them as facts. I can prove them to be so even in this country (Canada), by a cloud of living witnesses, and my readers will find that, instead of bringing absurd accusations against Her Grace, I have tried in some instances to screen her and her predecessors from the public hatred which their policy and the doings of their servants merited. Moreover, it is thirty years since I began to remonstrate with the House of Sutherland for their short-sighted policy in dealing with their people as they were doing, and it is twenty years since I began to expose them publicly with my real name, Donald MacLeod, attached to each letter, sending a copy of the public paper where it appeared, by post, to the Duke of Sutherland. These exposing and remonstrating letters were published in the Edinburgh papers, where the Duke and his predecessors had their principal Scottish law agent, and you can be assured that I was closely watched but they were unable to find one false accusation in my letters. I am well aware that each letter I have written on the subject would, if untrue, constitute a libel and I knew the editors, printers and publishers of these papers were as liable or responsible for libel as I was. But the House of Sutherland could never venture to raise an action of damages against either of us. In 1841, when I published my first pamphlet, I paid $4 50c. for binding one of them in splendid style and sent it by mail to His Grace the present Duke of Sutherland, with a complimentary note requesting him to peruse it and let me know if it contained anything offensive or untrue. I never received a reply, nor did I expect it; yet I am satisfied that His Grace did peruse it. I posted a copy of it to Mr. Loch, his chief commissioner; to Mr. W. Mackenzie, his chief lawyer in Edinburgh; to every one of their underlings, to sheep farmers and ministers in the county of Sutherland, who abetted the depopulators; and I challenged the whole of them and other literary scourges who aided and justified their unhallowed doings to contradict one statement I have made. Can you or any other believe that a poor sinner like Donald MacLeod would be allowed for so many years to escape with impunity had he been circulating and publishing calumnious, absurd falsehoods against such personages as the House of Sutherland? No, I tell you that if money could secure my punishment without establishing their own shame and guilt, it would be considered well spent long before now – they would eat me in penny pies if they could get me cooked for them.

I agree with you that the Duchess of Sutherland is a beautiful, accomplished lady who would shudder at the idea of taking a faggot or a burning torch in her hand to set fire to the cottages of her tenants, and so would her predecessor, the first Duchess of Sutherland, her good mother; likewise would the late and present Dukes of Sutherland. Yet it was done in their name, to their knowledge and with their sanction. The Dukes and Duchesses of Sutherland and those of their depopulating order have never had any call to defile their pure hands in burning people's houses; no, they have had plenty of willing tools at their beck to perform their dirty work. Whatever amount of humanity and purity of heart the late or the present Duke and Duchess may posses, we know the class of men from whom they selected their commissioners, factors and underlings. I knew every one of the unrighteous servants who ruled the Sutherland estate for the last fifty years and I am justified in saying that the most skilful phrenologist and physiognomist that ever existed could not discern one spark of humanity in the whole of them, from Mr. Loch down to Donald Sgrios. The most of those cruel executors of the atrocities I have been describing are now dead, and to be feared but not lamented. But it seems their chief was left to give you all the information you required about British slavery and oppression. I have read from speeches delivered by Mr. Loch at public dinners among his own party, that he would 'never be satisfied until the Gaelic language and the Gaelic people would be extirpated root and branch from the

Sutherland estate; yes, from the Highlands of Scotland.' He published a book where he stated as a positive fact that, when he got the management of the Sutherland estate, he found '408 families on the estate who never heard the name of Jesus' – whereas I could swear that there were not at that time, and for ages prior to it, more than two families within the limits of the county who did not worship that Name and Holy Being every morning and evening. I know there are hundreds in Canada who will bear me out in this assertion. I was at the pulling down and burning of the house of William Chisholm. I got my hands burned taking out the poor old woman from amidst the flames of her once-comfortable, though humble, dwelling, and a more horrifying and lamentable scene could scarcely be witnessed. I saw the skeleton of a once-tall, robust, high-cheekboned, respectable woman who had seen better days; who could neither hear, see, nor speak; without a tooth in her mouth, her cheek skin meeting in the centre, her eyes sunk out of sight in their sockets, her mouth wide open, her nose standing upright among smoke and flames, uttering piercing moans of distress and agony, in articulations from which could be only understood, '*Oh, Dhia, Dhia, teine, teine!*' (Oh, God, God, fire, fire.) When she came to the pure air, her bosom heaved to a most extraordinary degree, accompanied by a deep hollow sound from her lungs, comparable to the sound of thunder at a distance. When laid down upon the bare, soft, moss floor of the roofless shed, I will never forget the foam of perspiration which covered the pallid death-looking countenance. This was a scene, madam, worthy of an artist's pencil and of a conspicuous place on the stages of tragedy. Yet you call this a specimen of the ridiculous stories which found their way into respectable prints, because Mr. Loch, the chief factor, told you that Sellar, the head executive, brought an action against the sheriff and obtained a verdict for heavy damages. What a subterfuge; but it will not answer the purpose, '*the bed is too short to stretch yourself, and the covering too narrow and short to cover you.*' If you took the information and evidence upon which you founded your *Uncle Tom's Cabin* from such unreliable sources, who can believe the one-tenth of your novel? I cannot. I have at my hand here the grandchild of the slaughtered old woman, who remembers the events clearly. I have not far from me a respectable man, an elder in the Free Church, who was examined as a witness at Sellar's trial, at the Spring Assizes of Inverness in 1816, which you will find narrated in letters four and five of my work. Had you the opportunity, madam, of seeing the scenes which I, and hundreds more, have seen – the wild ferocious appearance of the infamous gang who constituted the burning party, their faces and hands covered with soot and ashes of the burning houses, cemented by torch-grease and their own sweat, kept continually drunk or half-drunk while at work; and to observe the hellish amusements some of them would get up for themselves and for an additional pleasure to their leaders! The people's houses were generally built upon slopes, and in many cases not far from pretty steep precipices. They preserved their meal in tight-made boxes and, when this fiendish party found any quantity of meal, they would carry it between them to the brink and dispatch it down the precipice amidst shrieks and yells. It was considered grand sport to see the box breaking to atoms and the meal mixed with the air. When they set fire to a house, they would watch any of the domestic animals making their escape from the flames, such as dogs, cats or any poultry; these were caught and thrown back to the flames – grand sport for demons in human form!

As to the vaunted letter, 'received from one of the most determined opposers of the measures, who travelled in the north of Scotland as editor of a newspaper, regretting all that he had written on the subject, being convinced that he was misinformed', I may tell you, madam, that this man did not travel to the north or in the north of Scotland, as editor. His name was Thomas Mulock; he came to Scotland a fanatic speculator in literature in search of money or a lucrative situation, vainly thinking that he would be a dictator to every editor in Scotland. He first attacked the immortal Hugh Miller of the *Witness,* Edinburgh, but in him he met more than his match. He then went to the North, got hold of my first pamphlet, and by setting it up in a literary style and in better English than I, he made a splendid and promising appearance in the northern papers for some

51

time, but he found out that the money expected was not coming in, and that the hotels, head inns and taverns would not keep him up any longer without the prospect of being paid for the past or the future. I found out that he was hard up, and a few of the Highlanders in Edinburgh and myself sent him from twenty to thirty pounds sterling. When he saw that that was all he was to get, he turned tail upon us and, instead of expressing his gratitude, he abused us unsparingly and regretted that ever he wrote on behalf of such a hungry, moneyless class. He smelled (like others we suspect) where the gold was hoarded up for hypocrites and flatterers and that one apologizing letter to His Grace would be worth ten times as much as he could expect from the Highlanders all his lifetime; and I doubt not it was, for his apology for the sin of misinformation got wide circulation.

He then went to France and started an English paper in Paris, and for the service he rendered Napoleon in crushing republicanism during the besieging of Rome, etc., the Emperor presented him with a *gold pin,* and in a few days afterwards sent a *gendarme* to him with a brief notice that his service was no longer required, and a warning to quit France in a few days. What became of him after I know not, but very likely he is dictating to young Loch, or some other Metternich.

No feelings of hostile vindictiveness, no desire to inflict chastisement, no desire to make riches influenced my mind, portraying the scenes of havoc and misery which in those past days darkened the annals of Sutherland. I write in my own humble style, with higher aims, wishing to prepare the way for demonstrating to the Dukes of Sutherland, and all other Highland proprietors great and small, that the path of selfish aggrandizement and oppression leads by sure and inevitable results to the ruin and destruction of the blind and misguided oppressors themselves. I consider the Duke himself victimized on a large scale by an incurably wrong system, and by being enthralled by wicked counsellors and servants. I have no hesitation in saying, had His Grace and his predecessors bestowed one-half of the encouragement they had bestowed upon strangers on the native inhabitants – a hardy, healthy, abstemious people, who lived peaceably in their primitive habitations, unaffected with the vices of a subtle civilization, possessing little, but enjoying much; a race devoted to their hereditary chief, ready to abide by his counsels; a race profitable in peace, and loyal, available in war – His Grace, the present Duke of Sutherland, and his beautiful Duchess, would be without compeers in the British dominions. Their rents would be at least doubled; would be as secure from invasion and annoyance in Dunrobin Castle as Queen Victoria could be in her Highland residence at Balmoral, and far safer than she is in her English home, Buckingham Palace; every man and son of Sutherland would be ready, as in the days of yore, to shed the last drop of their blood in defence of their chief, if required. Congratulations, rejoicings, dancing to the martial notes of the pipes, would meet them at the entrance to every glen and strath in Sutherlandshire, accompanied, surrounded and greeted as they proceeded, by the most grateful, devotedly attached, happy and bravest peasantry that ever existed. But there is nothing now, except desolation and the cries of famine and want, to meet the noble pair.

The ruins of once-comfortable dwellings will be seen, the landmarks of the furrows and ridges which yielded food to thousands, the footprints of the arch-enemy of human happiness, and ravage. Before, after and on each side are solitude, stillness and the quiet of the grave, disturbed only at intervals by the yells of a shepherd or foxhunter and the bark of a collie dog. Surely we must admit that the Marquises and Dukes of Sutherland have been duped and victimized to a most extraordinary and incredible extent, and we have Mr. Loch's own words for it in his speech in the House of Commons, 21st June, 1845: 'I can state as from facts that, from 1811 to 1833, not one sixpence of rent has been received from that county; on the contrary, there has been sent there for the benefit and improvement of the people a sum exceeding sixty thousand pounds sterling.' Now think you of this immense wealth which has been expended. I think the rental of the county would exceed £60,000 a year; you have then from 1811 to 1833, twenty-two years, leaving them at the above figures, and the sum total will amount to £1,320,000 expended upon the self-styled Sutherland improvements. Add to this £60,000 sent down to preserve the lives of the victims of those improvements from death by famine and the sum total will turn out in the shape of £1,380,000. It surely cost the heads of the House of Sutherland an immense sum of money to convert the county into the state I have described.

You should be surprised to hear and learn, madam, for what purposes most of the money drained from the Duke's coffers are expended since he became the Duke and proprietor of Sutherland, upholding the Loch policy. There are no fewer than seventeen who are known by the name of water bailiffs in the county, who receive yearly salaries, what doing, think you? Protecting the operations of the Loch policy, watching day and night the freshwater lakes, rivers and creeks, teeming with the finest salmon and trout fish in the world, guarding from the starving people, even during the years of famine and dire distress, when many had to subsist upon weeds, seaware and shellfish. The waters are preserved for the amusement of English anglers. Those dying from hunger are prevented from picking up any of the dead fish left by the sporting anglers rotting on the lake, creek and river sides when the smallest of them, or a morsel, would be considered by hundreds of them to be a treat. They dare not touch them, or if they do and are found out, they are imprisoned or removed summarily from His Grace's domains.

You will find, madam, that about three miles from Dunrobin Castle there is a branch of the sea which extends up the county about six miles, where mussels abound. Here you will find two sturdy men, mussel bailiffs, supplied with rifles and ammunition, and as many Newfoundland dogs as assistants, watching the mussel scalps, or beds, to preserve them from the people in the surrounding parishes of Dornoch, Rogart and Golspie. They keep the mussels to supply the fishermen on the opposite side of the Moray Firth with bait. These fishermen take away thousands of tons of this nutritive shellfish every year, when many hundreds of the people would be thankful for a daily diet of them, to pacify their hunger. You will find that the unfortunate native fishermen, who pay a yearly rent to His Grace for bait, are only permitted theirs from the refuse left by the strangers from the other side of the Moray Firth and, if they violate the *iron* rule laid down to them, they are entirely at the mercy of the underlings.

There has been an instance of two of the fishermen's wives who went on a cold, snowy, frosty day to gather bait but, on account of the boisterous sea, could not reach the place appointed by the factors. They took what they required from the forbidden ground, and were observed by the bailiffs, who pursued them like tigers. One came up to one of the women unobserved, took out his knife and cut the straps attaching the basket or creel on her back; the weight on her back fell to the ground, and she, poor woman, heavily pregnant, fell her whole length forward in the snow and frost. Her companion turned round to see what had happened and was pushed back with such force that she fell. The bailiff trampled their baskets and mussels to atoms, took them both prisoners, ordered one of them to call his superior bailiff to assist him and kept the other for two hours standing, cold and wet in the snow, until the superior came from three miles away. The two poor women were led, like convicted criminals, to Golspie, to appear before Lycurgus Gunn. They were left standing in front of their own doors in the snow until Marshall Gunn found it convenient to appear and pronounce judgment – verdict: You are allowed to go into your houses this night; this day week you must leave this village for ever and all the fishermen of the village are strictly prohibited from taking bait from the Little Ferry until you leave; my bailiffs are requested to see this my decree strictly attended to. As it was the middle of winter and there was heavy snow, they delayed a week longer: ultimately the villagers had to expel the two families from among them, as they depended upon the fishing for subsistence and they could not fish without bait.

This is a specimen of the injustice to and subjugation of the Golspie fishermen, and of the people at large; an example of the purposes for which the Duke's money is expended in that area. If you go, then, to the other side of the domain, you will find another Kyle, or a branch of the sea, which abounds in cockles and other shellfish, fortunately for the poor people. But in the years of distress, when the people were principally living upon vegetables, seaweed and shellfish, various diseases made their appearance amongst them hitherto unknown. The absence of meal of any kind being considered the primary cause, some of the people thought they would be permitted to exchange shellfish for meal with their more fortunate neighbours in Caithness, to whom such shellfish were a rarity. The Caithness boats came up loaded with meal, but the Loch embargo, through his underling in Tongue, who was watching their movements, was at once placed upon it; the Caithness boats had to return home with the meal and the Duke's people were left to their fate. Now, madam, you have steeped your brains and ransacked the English language to find refined terms for your panegyric on the Duke, Duchess and family of Sutherland. But I would briefly ask you (and others who devoted much of their time and talents in the same strain), would it not be more like a noble pair – if they did merit such noble praise as you have bestowed upon them – if they had, especially during years of famine and distress, freely opened up all these bountiful resources which God in His eternal wisdom and goodness prepared for His people, and which should never be intercepted nor restricted by man or men? You and others have composed hymns of praise, but it is questionable if there is a tune in heaven to sing them to.

> So I returned, and considered all the oppressions that
> are done under the sun: and behold the tears of such
> as were oppressed, and they had no comforter: and
> on the side of their oppressors there was power; but
> they had no comforter.
> *Ecclesiastes iv. I.*

> The wretch that works and weeps without relief
> Has one that notices his silent grief.
> He, from whose hands all pow'r proceeds
> Ranks its abuse among the foulest deeds,
> Considers *all* injustice with a frown,
> But *marks* the man that treads his fellow down.
> Remember Heav'n has an avenging rod –
> To smite the poor is treason against God.
> *Cowper.*

You shall find the Duke's money is expended for most astonishing purposes; much of it goes to hire hypocrites, and renowned literary flatterers, to vindicate the maladministration of those to whom he entrusted the management of his affairs and make his Grace (by nature a simple-minded man) believe his servants are innocent of all the charges brought against them and are doing justice to himself and to his people when they are doing the greatest injustice to both. Thus, instead of calling his servants to account at any time and enquiring into the broad charges brought against them – as every wise landlord should do – it seems the greater the enormities of foul deeds they commit, and the louder their accusations may sound through the land, the further he receives them into his favour. The fact is that James Loch was Duke of Sutherland, and not the 'tall, slender man with rather a thin face, light brown hair and mild blue eyes', who armed you up the extraordinary elegant staircase in Stafford House.

The Duchess of Sutherland pays a visit every year to Dunrobin Castle, and has seen and heard so many supplicating appeals presented to her husband by the poor fishermen of Golspie, soliciting liberty to take mussels from the Little Ferry Sands to bait their nets – a liberty of which they were deprived by his factors, though paying yearly rent for it. She answers on behalf of His Grace that he could do nothing for them. Can I believe that this is the same personage who can set out from Dunrobin Castle, her own Highland seat, and can ride in any direction for tens of miles, over fertile glens, valleys and straths, bursting with fatness, which gave birth to, and where were reared for ages, thousands of the bravest, the most moral, virtuous and religious men that Europe could boast of? They were once ready to a man, at a moment's warning from their chiefs, to rise in defence of their king, queen and country; animated with patriotism and love to their chief, and irresistible in the battle contest for victory. But these valiant men had then a *country,* a *home* and a *chief* worth the fighting for. She can now ride over these extensive tracts in the interior of the county without seeing the image of God upon a man travelling these roads, with the exception of a wandering Highland shepherd, wrapped up in a grey plaid to the eyes, with a collie dog behind him as a drill sergeant to train his ewes and to marshal his tups. There may happen to travel over the dreary tract a geologist, a tourist or a lonely carrier, but these are as rare as a pelican in the wilderness or a camel's convoy caravan in the deserts of Arabia. Add to this a few English sportsmen, with their stag hounds, pointer dogs and servants, and put themselves and the bravery together, and one company of French soldiers would put ten thousand of them to a disorderly flight, to save their own carcases, leaving their ewes and tups to feed the invaders!

Where have those people, who inhabited this country at one period, gone? In America and Australia the most of them will be found. The Sutherland family and the nation had no need of their services; hence they did not regard their patriotism or loyalty and disregarded their past services. Sheep, bullocks, deer and game became more valuable than men. Yet a remnant or, in other words, a *skeleton* of them is to be found along the seashore, huddled together in motley groups upon barren moors, among cliffs and precipices, in the most impoverished, degraded, subjugated, slavish, spiritless, condition that human beings could exist in. If this is really the lady who has 'Glory to God in the highest, peace on earth and good will to men' in view and who is so religiously denouncing the American statute which 'denies the slave the sanctity of marriage, with all its joys, rights, and obligations – which separates, at the will of the master, the wife from the husband, the children from the parents', I would advise her in God's name to take a tour round the sea-skirts of Sutherland, beginning at Brora, then to Helmsdale, Portskerra, Strath, Farr, Tongue, Durness, Edrachillis and Assynt, and learn the subjugated, degraded, impoverished, uneducated condition of the spiritless people of that sea-beaten coast, about two hundred miles in length. Let her with similar zeal remonstrate with her husband that their condition should be bettered; for the cure for all their misery and want is lying unmolested in the fertile valleys above, and all under his control. Let her advise His Grace, her husband, to be no longer guided by his Ahithophel, Mr. Loch, but to discontinue his depopulating schemes, which have separated many a wife from her husband, never to meet, which caused many a premature death and separated many sons and daughters, never to see each other. Let her persuade him to withdraw that mandate of Mr. Loch, which forbids marriage on the Sutherland estate, under pains and penalties of being banished from the county, for it has already augmented illegitimate connections and issues fifty per cent above what such were a few years ago, before this unnatural, ungodly law was put in force.

Let us see what the character of these ill-used people was! General Stewart of Garth, in his *Sketches of the Highlanders*, says: 'In the words of a general officer by whom the 93rd Sutherlanders were once reviewed, "They exhibit a perfect pattern of military discipline and moral rectitude. In the case of such men, disgraceful punishment would be as unnecessary as it would be pernicious." When the Sutherland Highlanders were stationed at the Cape of Good Hope they were anxious to enjoy the advantages of religious instruction agreeable to the tenets of their national church. There was no religious service in the garrison except the customary one of reading prayers to the soldiers on parade, so the Sutherland men formed themselves into a congregation, appointed elders of their own number, engaged and paid a stipend (collected among themselves) to a clergyman of the Church of Scotland and had divine service performed according to the ritual of the Established Church every Sabbath, and prayer meetings through the week.'

This reverend gentleman, Mr. Thom, in a letter which appeared in the *Christian Herald* of October, 1814, writes thus: 'When the 93rd Highlanders left Cape Town last month, there were among them 156 members of the church, including three elders and three deacons, all of whom, so far as men can know the heart from the life, were pious men. The regiment was certainly a pattern of morality and good behaviour to all other corps. They read their Bibles and observed the Sabbath. They saved their money to do good. Seven thousand rix-dollars, a sum equal to £1,200, the non-commissioned officers and privates saved for books, societies and for the spread of the Gospel, a sum unparalleled in any other corps in the world, given in the short space of eighteen months. Their example had a general good effect on both the colonists and the heathen. If ever apostolic days were revived in modern times on earth, I certainly believe some of those to have been granted to us in Africa.'

Another letter of a similar kind, addressed to the Committee of the Edinburgh Gaelic School Society (fourth annual report), says: 'The 93rd Highlanders arrived in England, when they immediately received orders to proceed to North America but, before they re-embarked, the sum collected for your society was made up and remitted to your treasurer, amounting to seventy-eight pounds, sterling.'

'In addition to this,' says the noble-minded, immortal General, 'such of them as had parents and friends in Sutherland did not forget their destitute condition, occasioned by the operation of the *fire and faggot*, mis-improved state of the county. During the short period the regiment was quartered at Plymouth, upwards of £500 was lodged in one banking house, to be remitted to Sutherland, exclusive of many sums sent through the Post Office and by officers, some of the sums exceeding £20 from an individual soldier. Men like these do credit to the peasantry of a country.

'It must appear strange, and somewhat inconsistent,' continues the General, 'when the same men who so loudly profess an eager desire to promote and preserve the religious and moral virtues of the people, so frequently take the lead in removing them from where they imbibed principles which have attracted the notice of Europe. The measures have lead to a deterioration, a system pregnant with degradation, poverty and disaffection.

'It is only when parents and heads of families in the Highlands are moral, happy and contented that they can instil sound principles into their children, who in their intercourse with the world may become what the men of Sutherland have already been, an honourable example, worthy of the imitation of all.'

At the commencement of the Russian war a correspondent wrote as follows:

'Your predictions are making their appearance at last, great demands are here for men to go to Russia, but they are not to be found. It seems that the Secretary of War has corresponded with all our

Highland proprietors, to raise as many men as they could for the Crimean War and ordered so many officers of rank to the Highlands to assist the proprietors in doing so, but it has been a complete failure as yet. The nobles advertised, by placards, meetings of the people. These proclamations were attended to but, when they came to understand what they were about, in most cases the recruiting proprietors and staff were saluted with the ominous cry of "Maa! maa! boo! boo!" and "Send your deer, your roes, your rams, dogs, shepherds and gamekeepers to fight the Russians, they have never done us any harm." The success of His Grace the Duke of Sutherland was deplorable; I believe you would have pitied the poor old man had you seen him.

'In my last letter I told you that his head commissioner and military officer, Mr. Loch, was in Sutherland for the last six weeks and failed in getting one man to enlist. On getting these doleful tidings, the Duke himself left London for Sutherland, arriving at Dunrobin about ten days ago. After presenting himself upon the streets of Golspie and Brora, he called a meeting of the male inhabitants of the parishes of Clyne, Rogart and Golspie. The meeting was well attended; upwards of 400 arrived at the appointed time; His Grace, with his military staff and factors, appeared shortly after. The people gave them a hearty cheer; His Grace took the chair. Three or four clerks took their seats at the table, and loosened down bulky packages of bank notes, and spread out platefuls of glittering gold. The Duke addressed the people very seriously and entered upon the necessity of going to war with Russia and the danger of allowing the Czar to have more power than what he holds already; of his cruel, despotic reign in Russia, etc. He praised the Queen and her government, rulers and nobles of Great Britain, who stood so much in need of men to put and keep down the tyrant of Russia, and foil him in his wicked schemes to take possession of Turkey. In concluding his address, which was often cheered, the Duke told the young able-bodied men that his clerks were ready to take down the names of all those willing to enlist. Every one who would enlist in the 93rd Highlanders would be given, there and then, £6 sterling. Those who would rather enter any other corps would get £3, all from his own private purse, independently of the government bounty. After advancing many silly flattering decoyments, he sat down to see the result, but there was no movement among the people. After sitting for a long time looking at the clerks, and they at him, his anxiety turned to indignation and he suddenly rose up and asked what was causing their non-attention to his proposals, but there was no reply. At last an old man, leaning upon his staff, moved towards the Duke and, when he approached near enough, he addressed His Grace as follows: "I am sorry for the response which Your Grace's proposals are meeting here today, so near the spot where your maternal grandmother, by giving forty-eight hours' notice, marshalled fifteen hundred men to pick out of them the nine hundred she required. But there is a cause for it, and a grievous cause and, as Your Grace demands to know it, I must tell you, as I see no one else is inclined in this assembly to do it. Your Grace's mother and predecessors applied to our fathers for men upon former occasions and our fathers responded to their call; they have made liberal promises, which neither they nor you performed. We are, we think, a little wiser than our fathers and we estimate your promises of today at the value of theirs. You should bear in mind that your predecessors and yourself expelled us in a most cruel and unjust manner from the land which our fathers held, in lien from your family, for their sons, brothers, cousins and relations, who were handed over to your parents to keep up their dignity, and to kill the Americans, Turks, French and Irish. These lands are devoted now to rear dumb brute animals, which you and your parents consider of far more value than men. I do assure Your Grace that it is the prevailing opinion in this county that, should the Czar of Russia take possession of Dunrobin Castle and of Stafford House next term, we could not expect worse treatment at his hands than we have experienced at the hands of your family for the last fifty years. Your parents, yourself and your commissioners have desolated the glens and straths of Sutherland, where you should find hundreds, yea, thousands of men to meet you and respond cheerfully to your call, had your parents and yourself kept faith with them. How could Your Grace expect to find men where they are not, and the few of them which are to be found among the rubbish or ruins of the county, have more sense than to be decoyed by chaff to the field of slaughter. But one comfort you have; though you cannot find men to fight, you can supply those who will fight with plenty of mutton, beef and venison." The Duke rose up, put on his hat, and left the field.'

It was the very reply His Grace deserved.

I know for a certainty this to be the prevailing feeling throughout the whole Highlands of Scotland, and who should wonder at it? How many thousands of them who served out their 21, 22, 25 and 26 years fighting for the British aristocracy, and on their return – wounded, maimed or worn out – to their own country, promising themselves to spend the remainder of their days in peace and enjoying the blessings and comfort their fathers enjoyed among their Highland, healthy, delightful hills, found to their grief that their parents were expelled from the country to make room for sheep, deer and game, the glens where they were born desolate and the abodes which sheltered them at birth and where they were reared to manhood burned to the ground? Instead of meeting the cheers, shaking hands, hospitality and affections of fathers, mothers, brothers, sisters and relations, they met with desolated glens, bleating of sheep, barking of dogs. If they should happen to rest their worn-out frame upon the green sod which has grown upon their father's hearth and a gamekeeper, factor or water bailiff came round, he would very unceremoniously tell them to absent themselves as smart as they could and not to annoy the deer. No race on record has suffered so much at the hands of those who should be their patrons, and proved to be so tenacious of patriotism as the Celtic race, but I assure you it has found its level now and will disappear soon altogether; and as soon as patriotism shall disappear in any nation, so sure that nation's glory is tarnished, victories uncertain, her greatness diminished and decaying consumptive death will be the result. If ever the old adage which says, 'Those whom the gods determine to destroy they first deprive them of reason,' was verified, it was and is in the case of the British aristocracy, and Highland proprietors in particular.

I am not so void of feeling as to blame the Duke of Sutherland, his parents or any other Highland absentee proprietor for all the evil done in the land but the evil was done in their name and under the authority they have invested in wicked, cruel servants. For instance, the only silly man who enlisted from among the great assembly which His Grace addressed was a married man, with three of a family and his wife. It was generally believed that his bread was baked for life. But no sooner was he away to Fort George to join his regiment than his home was pulled down. His wife and family were turned out and only permitted to live in a hut, in which an old female pauper had died a few days before. There the young family were sheltered and their names registered upon the poor roll for support; His Grace could not be guilty of such low rascality as this, yet he was told of it, but took no cognisance of those who did it in his name. It is likewise said that this man got a furlough of two weeks to see his wife and family before going abroad and that, when the factor heard he was coming, he ordered the ground officer of the parish of Rogart, named MacLeod, to watch the soldier and not allow him to see nor speak to his wife except in the officer's presence. We had at the same time, in the parish, an old bachelor of the name of John Macdonald, who had three idiot sisters, whom he supported, independent of any source of relief. A favourite of George, the notorious factor, envied this poor bachelor's farm, and he was summoned to remove at next term. The poor fellow petitioned His Grace and Loch, but to no purpose; he was doomed to walk away on the term-day, as the factor told him, 'to America, Glasgow, or to the devil if he choosed'. Seeing he had no other alternative, two days before the day of his removal he yoked his cart, got neighbours to help him to haul the three idiots into it and drove away with them to Dunrobin Castle. When he came up to factor Gunn's door, he capsized them out upon the green, wheeled about and went away home. The three idiots, finding themselves upon the top of one another so sudden, raised an inhuman-like yell, fixed into one another to fight and scratched, yelled and screeched so terrific that Mr. Gunn, his lady, his daughters and all the clerks and servants were soon about them; but they would not listen to reason, for they had none themselves, and continued their fighting and inharmonious music. Messenger after messenger was sent after John, but of no use; at last the great Gunn himself followed and overtook him, asked him how did he come to leave his sisters in such a state? He replied, 'I kept them while I had a piece of land to support them; you have taken that land from me, then take them along with the land, and make of them what you can; I must look out for myself but I cannot carry them to the labour market.' Gunn was in a fix, and had to give John assurance that he would not be removed if he would take his sisters, so John took them home and has not been molested as yet.

I have here beside me (in Canada) a respectable girl of the name of Ann Murray, whose father was removed during the time of the whole-sale *faggot* removals, but got a lot of a barren moor to cultivate. However barren-like it was, he was raising a family of industrious young sons, and by dint of hard labour and perseverance, they made it a comfortable home; but the young sons one by one left the country (and four of them are within two miles of where I sit). The result was that Ann was the only one who remained with the parents. The mother, who had an attack of palsy, was left entirely under Ann's care after the family left and she took it so much to heart that her daughter's attention was required day and night until death put an end to her afflictions after twelve years' suffering. Shortly after the mother's death, the father took ill and was confined to bed for nine months and Ann's labour re-commenced until his death. Though Ann Murray was the most dutiful of daughters, her incessant labour for a period of more than thirteen years made visible inroads upon her tender constitution. By the liberal assistance of her brothers, who did not lose sight of her and their parent (though upon a foreign strand), Ann Murray kept the farm in the best of order, no doubt expecting that she would be allowed to keep it after her parent's death, but this was not to be. The very day after her father's funeral, the officer came to her and told her that she was to be removed in a few weeks, that the farm was let to another and that Factor Gunn wished to see her. She was at that time afflicted with jaundice and told the officer she could not undertake the journey of ten miles. Next day the officer was at her again, more urgent than before, and made use of extraordinary threats, so she had to go. When she appeared before this Bashaw, he swore like a trooper and damned her soul for disobeying his first summons. She excused herself, trembling, that she was unwell; another volley of oaths and threats met her response, and he told her to remove herself from the estate next week for her conduct. She was issued with a threat not to take away nor sell a single article of furniture, implements of husbandry, cattle or crop. Nothing was allowed but her own body clothes; everything was to be handed over to her brother, who was to have the farm. Seeing there was neither mercy nor justice for her, she told him the crop, the house and every other thing belonging to the farm belonged to her and her brothers in America, that the brother to whom he (the factor) intended to hand over the farm and effects never helped her father or mother while in trouble and that she was determined that he should not enjoy what she laboured for, and what her other brothers paid for. She went and got the advice of a man of business, advertised a sale, sold off in the face of threats of interdict and came to Canada, where she was warmly received by brothers, sisters and friends now in Woodstock. No one could think nor believe that His Grace would ever countenance such doings as these but it was done in his name.

I have here within ten miles of me, Mr. William Ross, once taxman of Achtomleeny, Sutherlandshire, who occupied the most convenient farm to the principal deer-stalking hills in the county. Often have the English and Irish lords, connected in marriage with the Sutherlands, dined at William Ross's table and at his expense, and more than once passed the night under his roof. Mr. Ross was well acquainted with the mountains and haunts of the deer and was often engaged as a guide and instructor to these noblemen on their deer-stalking and fishing excursions. He became a real favourite with the Sutherland family, which enabled him to erect superior buildings to the common rule and improve his farm in a superior style; his mountainside farm was nothing short of a Highland paradise. But unfortunately for William, his nearest neighbour, one Major Gilchrist, a sheep farmer, coveted Mr. Ross's vineyard and tried many underhand schemes to secure the place for himself, but in vain. Ross would hearken to none of his proposals. But Ahab was a chief friend of Factor Gunn; and William Ross got notice of removal. Ross prepared a memorial to the first and late Duchess of Sutherland and placed it in her own hand. Her Grace read it, instantly went into the factor's office, told him that William Ross was not to be removed from Achtomleeny while he lived, wrote the same on the petition and handed it back to Ross with a graceful smile, saying, 'You are now out of the reach of factors; now, William, go home in peace.' William bowed and departed cheerfully but the factor and ground officer followed close behind him, and while Ross was reading Her Grace's deliverance, the officer, David Ross, came and snapped the paper out of his hand and ran to Factor Gunn with it. Ross followed but Gunn put it in his pocket, saying, 'William, you would need to give it to me afterwards at any rate, and I will keep it till I read it and then return it to you,' and, with a tiger-like smile on his face, said, 'I believe you came good speed today, and I am glad of it,' but William never got it in his hand again. However, he was not molested during Her Grace's life.

Next year she paid a visit to Dunrobin Castle, when Factor William Gunn advised Ross to apply to her for a reduction of rent, pretending to favour him. He did so, and it was granted cheerfully. Her Grace left Dunrobin that year, never to return; in the beginning of the next spring she was carried back to Dunrobin a corpse, and a few days after was interred at Dornoch. William Ross was served with a summons of removal from Achtomleeny and he had nothing to show. He petitioned the present Duke, and his commissioner, Mr. Loch, and related the whole circumstances to them, but to no avail, only he was told that Factor Gunn was ordered to give him some other lot of land, which he did. Having no other resource, William accepted it to his loss. Between loss of cattle and building and repairing houses, he had lost one hundred and fifty pounds sterling, from the time he was removed from Achtomleeny till he removed himself to Canada. He had a written agreement or promise for melioration or valuation for all the farm improvements and house building at Achtomleeny, which was valued by the family surveyor at two hundred and fifty pounds. William was always promised to get it, until they came to learn that he was leaving for America, then they would not give him a cent. William Ross left them with it to join his family in Canada, but he can in his old age sit at as comfortable a table and sleep on as comfortable a bed, with greater ease of mind and a clearer conscience, among his own dutiful and affectionate children, than the tyrant factor ever did, or ever will, among his. I know that this is but one or two cases out of the thousand I could enumerate, where the liberality and benevolence of His Grace and his parents were abused, and that to their patron's loss. You see in the above case that William was advised to plead for a reduction of rent, so that the factor's favourite, Ahab Gilchrist, would have the benefit of Naboth Ross's improvement, and the reduction he got on his rent, which would not be obtained otherwise.

The unhallowed crew of factors and officials, from the highest to the lowest grade, employed by the family of Sutherland, got the corrupt portion of the public press on their side to applaud their wicked doings and schemes as the only mode of improvement and civilization in the Highlands of Scotland. They have got what is still more to be lamented, all the Established ministers, with few exceptions, on their side and in them they found faithful auxiliaries in crushing the people. Any of them could hold a whole congregation by the hair of their heads over hell-fire, if they offered to resist the powers that be until they submitted. If a single individual resisted, he was denounced from the pulpit, and considered afterwards a dangerous man in the community and he might depart as quick as he could. Any man may violate the laws of God and the laws of heaven as often as he chooses – he is never heeded and has nothing to fear – but if he offends the Duke's factor, the lowest of his minions, or violates the least of their laws and regulations, it is an unpardonable sin. The present Duke's mother was no doubt a liberal lady of many good parts and seemed to be much attached to the natives but, unfortunately for them, she employed as factors a vile, unprincipled crew, who were their avowed enemies. She would hear the complaints of the people and would write to the ministers of the Gospel to ascertain the correctness of complaints, and the factor was justified, however gross the outrage that he committed. The minister dined with the factor and could not refuse to favour him. The present Duke is a simple, narrow-minded gentleman, who concerns himself very little even about his own pecuniary affairs; he entrusts his whole affairs to his factors and the people are enslaved so much that it is now considered the most foolish thing a man can do to petition His Grace, whatever is done to him, for it will go hard with the factor, or he will punish and make an example of him to deter others.

When a marriage in the family of Sutherland takes place, or the birth of an heir, a feast is ordered for the Sutherland people, consisting of whisky, porter, ale and plenty of eatables. The day of feasting and rejoicing is appointed and heralded throughout the country, and the people are enjoined in martial terms to assemble. Barrels of raw and adulterated whisky are forwarded to each parish, some raw adulterated sugar, and that is all. Bonfires are prepared on the tops of the highest mountains. The poorest of the poor are warned by family officers to carry the materials, consisting of peats and tar barrels, upon their backs. The scene is lamentable, to see groups of these wretched, half-clad and ill-shod people climbing up these mountains with their loads. The work must be done, there is no denial, the evening of rejoicing is arrived and the people are assembled at their different clachans. The barrels of whisky are taken out to the open field, poured into large tubs, a good amount of abominable-looking sugar is mixed with it and a sturdy favourite is employed to stir it about with a flail handle or some long cudgel — all sorts of drinking implements are produced, tumblers, bowls, ladles and tin jugs. Bagpipers are set up with great glee. In the absence of the factor, the animal called the ground officer, and in some instances the parish minister, will open the jollification and show an example to the people of how to deal with this coarse beverage. After the first round, the respectable portion of the people will depart or retire to an inn where they can enjoy themselves but the *drouthies* and ignorant youth will keep the field of revelling until tearing of clothes and faces comes to be the rule. Fists and cudgels supplant jugs and ladles, and this will continue until king Bacchus enters the field and hushes the most heroic brawlers and the most ferocious combatants to sound snoring on the field of rejoicing, where many of them enter into contracts with death, from which they could never extricate themselves. With the co-operation and assistance of factors, ministers and editors, a most flourishing account is sent to the world, and to the absentee family in London, who knows nothing about how the affair was conducted. The world will say how happy must the people be who live under such good and noble, liberal-minded patrons; the patrons themselves are so highly pleased with the report that, however extraordinary the bill that comes to them on the rent day in place of money – for roast beef and mutton, bread and cheese, London porter and Edinburgh ale which was never bought nor tasted by the people – they will consider their commissioners used great economy; the bill is accepted and discharged, the people are deceived and the proprietors injured.

CHAPTER II

ROSS-SHIRE

Glencalvie

Great cruelties were perpetrated at Glencalvie, Ross-shire, where the evicted had to retire into the parish churchyard. There for more than a week they found the only shelter obtainable in their native land. No one dared help them, under threat of receiving similar treatment to those thus driven among the tombs. Many of them, indeed, wished that their lot had landed them under the sod with their ancestors and friends, rather than be treated and driven out of house and home in such a ruthless manner. A special commissioner sent down by the London *Times* describes the circumstances as follows:

Those who remember the misery and destitution into which large masses of the population were thrown by the systematic Clearances carried on in Sutherlandshire some twenty years ago, under the direction and on the estate of the late Marchioness of Stafford will regret to learn that the heartless scourge, with all its sequences of misery, destitution and crime, is again being resorted to in Ross-shire. Amongst an imaginative people like the Highlanders, poetic from dwelling amongst wild and romantic scenery, it requires little, with fair treatment, to make them almost idolize their heritor. They would spend the last drop of their blood in his service. But this feeling of respectful attachment to the landowners, which money cannot buy, is fast passing away.

This change is not without cause and perhaps – if the dark deeds of calculating 'feelosophy' carried out by factors in some of these lonely glens, the almost inconceivable misery and hopeless destitution in which, for the promise of a few pounds, hundreds of peaceable, generally industrious and contented peasants are driven out from the means of self-support to become wanderers and starving beggars, and in which a brave and valuable population is destroyed, are exposed to the gaze of the world – general indignation and disgust may effect what moral obligations and humanity cannot. One of these Clearances is about to take place in the parish of Kincardine and throughout the whole district it has created the strongest feeling of indignation.

This parish is divided into two districts, each of great extent: one is called the parliamentary district of Croick. The length of this district is about twenty miles, with a breadth of from ten to fifteen miles. It extends amongst the most remote and unfrequented parts of the country, consisting chiefly of hills of heather and rock, peopled only in a few straths and glens. This district was formerly thickly peopled but one of those Clearances many years ago nearly swept away the population and now the whole number of its inhabitants amounts, I am told, to only three hundred and seventy souls. These live in three straths, or glens, called Amatnatua, Greenyard and Glencalvie. It is the inhabitants of Glencalvie, some ninety people, whose turn it is now to be turned out of their homes, all at once, the aged and the helpless as well as the young and strong, nearly all without hope for the future. The proprietor of this glen is Major Charles Robertson of Kindeace, who is at present with his regiment in Australia. His factor, or steward, who acts for him in his absence, is Mr. James Gillanders of Highfield Cottage, near Dingwall. Glencalvie is situated about twenty-five miles east of Tain. Bleak rough hills, whose surfaces are almost all rock and heather, close in on all sides, leaving in the valley a gentle slope of arable land of a very poor description, dotted over by cairns of stone and rock, not more than fifteen to twenty acres in extent. For this piece of indifferent land with a right of pasturage on the hills impinging upon it – and on which, if it were not a fact that sheep do live, you would not credit that they could live, so entirely does it seem void of vegetation, aside from the brown heather, whilst its rocky nature makes it dangerous and impossible even for a sheep

72

walk – the almost unbelievable rent of £55 10s. has been paid. I am convinced that for the same land no farmer in England would give £15 at the utmost.

Even respectable farmers here say they do not know how the people raise the rent for it. Potatoes and barley were grown in the valley, and some sheep and a few black cattle find provender amongst the heather. Eighteen families have each a cottage in the valley; they have always paid their rent punctually and have contrived to support themselves in all ordinary seasons. They have no poor on the poor roll, and they help one another over the winter. I am told that not an inhabitant of this valley has been charged with any offence for years back. During the war it furnished many soldiers; and an old pensioner, eighty-two years of age, who has served in India, is now dying in one of these cottages, where he was born. For the convenience of the proprietor, some ten years ago, four of the principal tenants became responsible for the rest, collecting all the rents and paying the whole in one sum.

The Clearance of this valley, having attracted much notice, has been thoroughly enquired into, and a kind of defence has been entered upon respecting it, which I am told has been forwarded to the Lord Advocate. Thanks to Mr. Mackenzie, writer, Tain, I have been favoured with a copy of it. The only explanation or defence of the Clearance that I can find in it is that, shortly after Mr. Gillanders assumed the management of Major Robertson's estate, he found that it became absolutely necessary to adopt a different system in regard to the lands of Glencalvie 'from that hitherto pursued'.

The 'different system' was to turn the barley and potato grounds into a sheep walk, and the 'absolute necessity' for it is an alleged increase of rent.

It was, accordingly, in 1843, attempted to serve summonses of removal upon the tenants. They were in no arrears of rent, they had no burdens in poor; for 500 years their fathers had peaceably occupied the glen and the people were naturally indignant. Who can be surprised that, when the constables went amongst them with the summonses, they acted in a manner which, while it showed their excitement, not the less demonstrated their wish to avoid breaking the law? The women met the constables beyond the boundaries, over the river and seized the hand of the one who held the notices; whilst some held it out by the wrist, others held a live coal to the papers and set fire to them. They were afraid of being charged with destroying the notices and sought in this way to evade the consequences. This act of resistance has been made the most of. One of the men told me, hearing they were to be turned out because they did not pay rent enough, that they offered to pay £15 a year more, and afterwards to pay as much rent as any other man would give for the place. The following year (1844), the four chief tenants were summoned to Tain, under the assurance that Mr. Gillanders was going to settle with them, and believing that their holdings were to be continued to them. The notices were then, as they say, in a treacherous and tricky manner, served upon them. Having been served, 'a decreet of removal' was obtained against them, under which, if they refused to turn out, they would be put out by force. Finding themselves in this position, they entered into an arrangement with Mr. Gillanders, in which after several propositions on either side, it was agreed that they should remain until the 12th May, to give them time to provide themselves with holdings elsewhere. Mr. Gillanders agreed to pay them £100 on quitting, and to take their stock on at a valuation. They were also to be free to carry away the timber of their houses, which was really worthless except for firewood. On their part they agreed to leave peaceably and not to lay down any crop. Beyond the excessive harshness of removing the people at all, it is only fair to say that the method of proceeding in the removal up until now has been temperate and considerate.

Two respectable farmers became responsible for the people, to ensure that they would carry out their part of the agreement, and the time of removal has since been extended to the 25th of this month. In the defence got up for this proceeding it is stated that all have been provided for; this is not only not the case, but seems to be intentionally deceptive. In speaking of all, the four principal tenants only are meant, for, according to the factor, these were all he had any

74

dealings with. Even in regard to the four principal tenants, it is not the case. Two only, a father and son, have got a piece of black moor near Tain, twenty-five miles off, without any house or shed on it, out of which they hope to obtain subsistence. For this they are to pay £1 rent for seven acres the first year, £2 for the second year and £3 for a continuation. Another old man with a family has a house and a small lot of land in Edderton, about twenty miles off. These three are the only ones who have obtained places where they may hope to make a living. The old pensioner, if removing does not kill him, has obtained for himself and family, and his son's family, a house at a rent of £3 or £4, some ten miles off, without any land or means of subsistence attached to it. This old soldier has been offered 2s. a week by the factor to support him while he lives. He was one of the four principal tenants responsible for the rent and he indignantly refused to be kept as a pauper.

A widow with four children, two imbecile, has two small apartments in a bothy, or turf hut, near Bonar Bridge, for which she is to pay £2 rent, without any land or means of subsistence. Another, a man with a wife and four children, has an apartment at Bonar Bridge, at £1 rent. He goes there quite destitute, without means of living. Six only of eighteen households, therefore, have been able to obtain places in which to put their heads and, of these, three only have any means of subsistence before them. The rest are hopeless and helpless. Two or three of the men told me they have been round to every factor and proprietor in the neighbourhood and they could obtain no place and nothing to do, and they did not know where to go or what to do to live.

And for what are all these people to be reduced from comfort to beggary? For what is this virtuous and contented community to be scattered? I confess I can find no answer. It is said that the factor would rather have one tenant than many, as it saves him trouble! But so long as the rent is punctually paid, as it has been, it goes against experience to suppose that one large tenant will pay more rent than many small ones, or that a sheep walk can pay more rent than culti-vated land.

Let me add that, so far from the Clearance at Glencalvie being a solitary instance in this neighbourhood, it is one of many. The tenants of Newmore, near Tain, who I am told, amount to sixteen families, are to be 'weeded out' on the 25th, by the same Mr. Gillanders. The same factor manages the Strathconon estate, about thirty miles from Newmore, from which, during the last four years, some hundreds of families have been weeded. The Government Church of that district, built eighteen years ago, to meet the necessities of the people, is now almost unnecessary from the want of population. At Black Isle, near Dingwall, the same agent is pursuing the same course, and so strong is the feeling of the poor Highlanders at these outrageous proceedings, so far as they are concerned wholly unwarranted from any cause whatever, that I am informed on the best authority, and by those who go amongst them and hear what they say, that it is owing to the influence of religion alone that they refrain from breaking out into open and turbulent resistance of the law. I enclose you the defence of this proceeding, with a list of the names and numbers of each family in Glencalvie – in all, ninety-two persons.

London *Times*, Tuesday, 20th May, 1845.

The Eviction of the Rosses of Glencalvie

In a 'Sermon for the Times', the Rev. Richard Hibbs of the Episcopal Church, Edinburgh, referring to these evictions, says:

'Take first the awful proof how far in oppression men can go – men highly educated and largely gifted in every way – property, talents, all; for the most part indeed, they are so-called noblemen. What, then, are they doing in the Highland districts, according to the testimony of a learned professor in this city? Why, depopulating those districts in order to make room for red deer. And how? By buying off the cottars, and giving them money to emigrate? Not at all, but by starving them out; by rendering them absolutely incapable of procuring subsistence for themselves and families, for they first take away from them their apportionments of poor lands, although they may have paid their rents. If that don't suffice to eradicate from their hearts that love of the soil on which they have been born and bred, why, then, these inhuman landlords, who are far more merciful to their beasts, take away from these poor cottars the very roofs above their defenceless heads and expose them, worn down with age and destitute of everything, to the inclemencies of a northern sky; and this because they must have plenty room for their dogs and deer. For plentiful instances of the most wanton barbarities under this head, we need only point to the Knoydart evictions. Here were perpetrated such enormities as might well have caused the very sun to hide his face at noon-day.'

Macleod, referring to Hibbs's 'Sermon for the Times', says:

'It has been intimated to me by an individual who heard this discourse on the first occasion that the statements referring to the Highland landlords have been controverted. I was well aware, long before the receipt of this intimation, that some defence had appeared, and here I can truly say that none would have rejoiced more than myself to find that a complete vindication had been made. But, unhappily, the case is far otherwise. In order to be fully acquainted with all that had passed on the subject, I have put myself during the week in communication with the learned professor to whose letter, which appeared some months ago in the *Times*, I referred. From him I learn that none of his statements were invalidated and he adds that to do this was simply impossible, as he had been at great pains to verify the facts. All that could be called in question was the theory that he had based upon those facts – namely, that evictions were made for the purpose of making room for more deer. This, of course, was open to contradiction on the part of those landlords who had not openly stated their reason for evicting the poor Highland families. As to the evictions themselves, no attempt at contradiction was made.'

'I hold in my hand,' Mr. Hibbs continued, 'a little work entitled "The Massacre of the Rosses", which has passed into the second edition. The author, Mr. Donald Ross – is a gentleman whom all who feel sympathy for the downtrodden and oppressed must highly esteem. What a humiliating picture of the barbarity and cruelty of fallen humanity does this little book present! The reader, utterly appalled by its horrifying statements, finds it difficult to retain the rec-ollection that he is reading the history of his own times and country. He would rather succumb to the tempting illusion that the ruthless atrocities which are depicted were enacted in a fabulous period, in ages long past or, at least, that the scene of such heartrending cruel-ties, the perpetrators of which were regardless alike of the innocency of infancy and the helplessness of old age, is some far distant and, as yet, not merely unchristianized, but wholly savage and uncivilized, region of our globe. But, alas! it is Scotland, in the latter half of the nineteenth century, of which he writes. One feature of the heart-harrowing case is the shocking and barbarous cruelty that was prac-tised on this occasion upon the women of the evicted clan.

'Mr. Ross, in a letter addressed to the Right Hon. the Lord Advo-cate, Edinburgh, dated 19th April, 1854, thus writes in reference to one of those clearances and evictions which had just then taken place, under the authority of a certain Sheriff of the district, and by means of a body of policemen as executioners: "The feeling on this subject, not only in the district, but in Sutherlandshire and Ross-shire, is, among the great majority of the people, one of universal condemna-tion of the Sheriff's reckless conduct, and of indignation and disgust at the brutality of the policemen. Such, indeed, was the sad havoc made on the women on the banks of the Carron, on the memorable 31st March last, that pools of blood were on the ground, that the dogs of the district came and licked up the blood and, at last, such was the state of feeling of parties who went from a distance to see the field that a party (it is understood, by order from headquarters) actu-ally harrowed the ground during the night to hide the blood!

'"The affair at Greenyard, on the morning of the 31st March last, is not calculated to inspire much love of country or rouse the martial spirit of the already ill-used Highlanders. The savage treatment of innocent women on that morning by an enraged body of police throws the Sinope butchery into the shade; for the Ross-shire Haynaus have shown themselves more cruel and more bloodthirsty than the Austrian women-floggers. What could these poor men and women – with their wounds and scars, and broken bones, and disjointed

78

arms, stretched on beds of sickness, or moving on crutches, the result of the brutal treatment of them by the police at Greenyard – have to dread from the invasion of Scotland by Russia?'"

Commenting on this incredible atrocity, committed in the middle of the nineteenth century, Donald Macleod says truly, 'It was so horrifying and brutal that he did not wonder at the Rev. gentleman's delicacy in speaking of it and directing his hearers to peruse Mr. Ross's pamphlet for full information. Mr. Ross went all the way from Glasgow to Greenyard, to investigate the case upon the spot, and found that Mr. Taylor, a native of Sutherland, well educated in the evicting schemes and murderous cruelty of that county, and Sheriff-Substitute of Ross-shire, marched from Tain on the morning of the 31st March, at the head of a strong party of armed constables, with heavy bludgeons and firearms conveyed in carts and other vehicles, allowing them as much strong drink as they chose to take before leaving and on their march, to prepare them for the bloody work which they had to perform; fit for any outrage, fully equipped, and told by the Sheriff to show no mercy to anyone who would oppose them, and not allow themselves to be called cowards, by allowing these mountaineers victory over them. In this excited, half-drunken state, they came in contact with the unfortunate women of Greenyard, who were determined to prevent the officers from serving the summonses of removal upon them, and keep their holding of small farms where they and their forefathers lived and died for generations. But no time was allowed for talk; the Sheriff gave the order to clear the way, and, to his everlasting disgrace, he struck the first blow at a woman, the mother of a large family, and large in the family way at the time, who tried to keep him back. Then a general slaughter commenced; the women made noble resistance until the bravest of them got their arms broken and they gave way. This did not allay the rage of the murderous brutes, who continued clubbing at the helpless creatures until every one of them was stretched on the field, weltering in their blood, or with broken arms and ribs and bruised limbs. In this woeful condition many of them were handcuffed together, others tied with coarse ropes, huddled into carts, and carried prisoners to Tain. I have

79

seen myself in the possession of Mr. Ross, Glasgow, patches or scalps of the skin with the long hair adhering to them, found on the field a few days after this inhuman affray. I did not see the women but I was told that gashes were found on the heads of two young female prisoners in Tain jail, which exactly corresponded to the slices of scalps which I have seen. Mr. Donald Ross placed the whole affair before the Lord Advocate for Scotland but no notice was taken of it by that functionary, further than that the majesty of the law would need to be observed and attended to.

'In this unfortunate country, the law of God and humanity may be violated and trampled underfoot, but the law of wicked men which sanctions murder, rapine, and robbery must be observed. From the same estate (the estate of Robertson of Kindeace, if I am not mistaken in the date), in the year 1843, the whole inhabitants of Glencalvie were evicted in a similar manner. So unprovided and unprepared were they for removal at such an inclement season of the year that they had to shelter themselves in a church and a burying-ground. I have seen myself nineteen families within this gloomy and solitary resting abode of the dead. They were there for months. The London *Times* sent a commissioner direct from London to investigate this case and he did his duty but, like the Sutherland cases, it was hushed up in order to maintain the majesty of the law and to keep the right, the majesty of the people and the laws of God in the dark.

'In the year 1819 or 1820, about the time when the depopulation of Sutherlandshire was completed and the annual burning of the houses ceased and when there was not a glen or strath in the county to let to a sheep farmer, one of these insatiable monsters of Sutherlandshire sheep farmers fixed his eyes upon a glen in Ross-shire, inhabited by a brave, hardy race from time immemorial. Summonses of removal were served upon them at once. The people resisted and a military force was brought against them. The military and the women of the glen met at the entrance to the glen and a bloody conflict took place. Without reading the riot act or taking any other precaution, the military fired (by the order of Sheriff MacLeod) ball cartridge upon the women. One young girl of the name of

Mathieson was shot dead on the spot; many were wounded. When this murder was observed by the survivors and some young men concealed in the background, they made a heroic sudden rush upon the military and a hand-to-hand fight took place. In a few minutes the military were put to disorder by flight; in their retreat they were unmercifully dealt with, only two of them escaping with whole heads. The Sheriff's coach was smashed to atoms and he made a narrow escape himself with a whole head. But no legal cognisance was taken of this affair, as the Sheriff and the military were the violators. However, for fear of prosecution, the Sheriff settled a pension of £6 sterling yearly upon the murdered girl's father and the case was hushed up. The result was that the people kept possession of the glen, and the proprietor and the oldest and most insatiable of Sutherlandshire scourges went to law, which ended in the ruination of the latter, who died a pauper.'

Hugh Miller, describing a 'Highland Clearing' in one of his able leading articles in the *Witness,* quotes freely from an article by John Robertson, which appeared in the *Glasgow National* in August, 1844, on the evictions of the Rosses of Glencalvie. When the article from which Hugh Miller quotes was written, the inhabitants of the glen had received notices of removal but the evictions had not yet been carried out. Commenting on the proceedings, Hugh Miller says:

'In an adjacent glen (to Strathcarron), through which the Calvie works its headlong way to the Carron, that terror of the Highlanders, a summons of removal, has been served within the last few months on a whole community and Mr. Robertson relates graphically both the peculiar circumstances in which it has been issued and the feelings which it has excited. We find from his testimony that the old state of things which is so immediately on the eve of being broken up in this locality, lacked not a few of those sources of terror to the proprietary of the county that are becoming so very formidable to them in the newer states.'

'The constitution of society in the Glens,' says Mr. Robertson, 'is remarkably simple. Four heads of families are bound for the whole rental. The number of souls was about ninety, sixteen cottages paid

81

rent; they supported a teacher for the education of their own children; they supported their own poor. The laird has never lost a farthing of rent in bad years, such as 1836 and 1837; the people may have required the favour of a few weeks' delay, but they are not now a single farthing in arrears; that is, when they are in receipt of summonses of removal.

'For a century,' Mr. Robertson continues, speaking of the Highlanders, 'their privileges have been lessening; they dare not now hunt the deer, or shoot the grouse or the blackcock; they have no longer the range of the hills for their cattle and their sheep; they must not catch a salmon in the stream; in earth, air and water, the rights of the laird are greater, and the rights of the people are smaller, than they were in the days of their forefathers.' The same writer eloquently concludes:

'The father of the laird of Kindeace bought Glencalvie. It was sold by a Ross two short centuries ago. The swords of the Rosses of Glencalvie did their part in protecting this little glen, as well as the broad lands of Pitcalvie, from the ravages and the clutches of hostile septs. These clansmen bled and died in the belief that every principle of honour and morals secured their descendants a right to subsisting on the soil. The chiefs and their children had the same charter of the sword. Some Legislatures have made the right of the people superior to the right of the chief; British lawmakers made the rights of the chief everything, and those of their followers nothing. The ideas of the morality of property are in most men the creatures of their interests and sympathies. Of this there cannot be a doubt, however; the chiefs would not have had the land at all could the clansmen have foreseen the present state of the Highlands – their children in mournful groups going into exile, the faggot of legal myrmidons in the thatch of the feal cabin, the hearths of their homes and their lives the green sheep walks of the stranger. Sadly, it is seemingly the will of our constituencies that our laws shall prefer the few to the many. Most mournful will it be, should the clansmen of the Highlands have been cleared away, ejected, exiled in deference to a political, moral, social and economical mistake – a suggestion not of philosophy but of

Mammon – a system in which the demon of sordidness assumed the shape of the angel of civilization and of light.'

That the Eviction of the Rosses was of a harsh character is amply corroborated by the following account, extracted from the *Inverness Courier*.

'We mentioned last week that considerable obstruction was anticipated in the execution of the summonses of removal upon the tenants of Major Robertson of Kindeace on his property of Greenyard, near Bonar Bridge. The office turned out to be of a very formidable character. At six o'clock on the morning of Friday last, Sheriff Taylor proceeded from Tain, accompanied by several Sheriff officers and a police force of about thirty more, partly belonging to the constabulary force of Ross-shire and partly to that of Inverness-shire, the latter under the charge of Mr. Mackay, inspector, Fort William. On arriving at Greenyard, nearly four miles from Bonar Bridge, it was found that about three hundred persons, two-thirds of whom were women, had assembled from the county round about, all apparently prepared to resist the execution of the law. The women stood in front, armed with stones, and the men occupied the background, all, or nearly all, furnished with sticks.

'The Sheriff attempted to reason with the crowd and to show them the necessity of yielding to the law but his efforts were fruitless; some of the women tried to lay hold of him and strike him and, after a painful effort to effect the object in view by peaceable means – which was renewed in vain by Mr. Cumming, the superintendent of the Ross-shire police – the Sheriff was reluctantly obliged to employ force. The force was led by Mr. Cumming into the crowd and, after a sharp resistance, which lasted only a few minutes, the people were dispersed and the Sheriff was enabled to execute the summonses upon the four tenants. The women, as they bore the brunt of the battle, were the principal sufferers. A large number of them – fifteen or sixteen, we believe – were seriously hurt and, of these, several are under medical treatment; one woman, we believe, still lies in a precarious condition. The policemen appear to have used their batons with great force, but they escaped themselves almost unhurt. Several

correspondents from the district, who do not appear to make sufficient allowance for the critical position of affairs and the necessity of
at once impressing so large a multitude with the serious nature of the
case, complain that the policemen used their batons with wanton
cruelty. Others state that they not only did their duty but that less
firmness might have proved fatal to themselves. The instances of violence are certainly, though very naturally, on the part of the attacking
force; several batons were smashed in the melee; a great number of
men and women were seriously hurt, especially about the head and
face, while not one of the policemen, so far as we can learn, suffered
any injury. As soon as the mob was fairly dispersed, the police made
active pursuit in the hope of catching some of the ringleaders. The
men had, however, fled and the only persons apprehended were some
women who had been active in the opposition and who had been
wounded. They were conveyed to the prison at Tain but liberated on
bail next day through the intercession of a gallant friend, who became responsible for their appearance.

'A correspondent writes,' continues the *Courier*, 'that ten young
women were wounded in the back of the skull and other parts of
their bodies . . . The wounds on these women show plainly the severe
manner in which they were dealt with by the police when they were
retreating. It was reported last night that one of them was dead and
the feeling of indignation is so strong against the manner in which
the constables have acted that I fully believe the life of any stranger, if
he were supposed to be an officer of the law, would not be worth
twopence in the district.'

The *Northern Ensign*, referring to the same case, says:

'One day lately a preventive officer with two cutter men made
their appearance on the boundaries of the estate and were taken for
Tain Sheriff officers. The signals were at once given and in course of
half-an-hour the poor gauger and his men were surrounded by three
hundred men and women, who would not listen to reason either in
English or Gaelic; the poor fellows were taken and denuded of their
clothing, all papers and documents were extracted and burned,
amongst which was a purse with a considerable quantity of money.

In this state they were carried shoulder-high off the estate, and left at the braes of Downie, where the great Culrain riot took place thirty years ago.'

Kintail

During the first years of the century a great many were cleared from Kintail by Seaforth at the instigation of his Kintail factor, Duncan Mor Macrae, and his father, who themselves added the land taken from the ancient tenantry to their own already extensive sheep farms. In Glengarry, Canada, a few years ago, we met one man, ninety-three years of age, who was among the evicted. He was in excellent circumstances, his three sons having three valuable farms of their own, and considered wealthy in the district. In the same county there is a large colony of Kintail men, the descendants of those cleared from that district, all comfortable or well off, one of them being then member for his county in the dominion Parliament. While this has been the case with many of the evicted from Kintail and their descendants in Canada, the grasping sheep farmer who was the original cause of their eviction from their native land, died ruined and penniless and the Seaforths, not long after, had to sell the last inch of their ancient inheritance in Lochalsh and Kintail. Shortly after these Glenelchaig evictions, about fifty families were banished in the same way and by the same people from the district of Letter-fearn. This property has also changed hands since, and is now in possession of Sir Alexander Matheson, Baronet of Lochalsh. Letter of Lochalsh was cleared by Sir Hugh Innes almost as soon as he came into possession by purchase of that portion of the ancient heritage of Seaforth and Kintail. The property has since passed into the hands of the Lillingstones.

Coigeach

The attempt to evict the Coigeach crofters must also be mentioned. Here the people made a stout resistance, the women disarming about twenty policemen and Sheriff officers, burning the summonses in a heap, throwing their batons into the sea, and ducking the representatives of the law in a neighbouring pool. The men formed the second line of defence, in case the women should receive any ill-treatment. They, however, never put a finger on the officers of law, all of whom returned home without serving a single summons or evicting a single crofter. The proceedings of her subordinates fortunately came to the ears of the noble proprietrix, with the result that the Coigeach tenants are still where they were, and are today among the most comfortable crofters in the north of Scotland.

Strathconon

From 1840 to 1848 Strathconon was almost entirely cleared of its ancient inhabitants to make room for sheep and deer and for extensive forest plantations. The property was under trustees when the harsh proceedings were commenced by the factor, Mr. Rose, a notorious Dingwall solicitor.

He began by taking away, first, the extensive hill pasture, for generations held as club farms by the townships, thus reducing the people from a position of comfort and independence and, secondly, as we saw done elsewhere, evicting them from the arable portion of the strath, though they were not a single penny in arrear of rent. Coirre-Bhuic and Scard-Roy were first cleared, and given, respectively, as sheep farms, to Mr. Brown from Morayshire and Colin Munro from Dingwall. Mr. Balfour, when he came of age, cleared Coire-Feola and Achadh-an-eas. Carnach was similarly treated, while no fewer than twenty-seven families were evicted from Glen-Meine alone. Baile-a-Mhuilinn and Baile-na-Creige were cleared in 1844, at least twenty-four families from these townships removing to the neighbourhood of Knock-farrel and Loch Ussie, above Dingwall, where they were provided with holdings by the late John Hay Mackenzie of Cromarty, father of the present Duchess of Sutherland, and where a few of themselves and many of their descendants are now in fairly comfortable circumstances. A great many more found shelter on various properties in the Black.

It is computed that four to five hundred souls were thus driven from Strathconon and cast adrift on the world, including a large number of persons quite helpless from old age, blindness and other infirmities. The scenes were much the same as we have described in connection with other places. There is, however, one aspect of the harshness and cruelty practised on the Strathconon people not applicable in many other cases, namely, that in most instances where they settled down and reclaimed land, they were afterwards re-evicted and the lands they had brought into cultivation taken from them without any compensation whatever, and given at enhanced rents to large farmers. This is specially true of those who settled down in the Black Isle, where they reclaimed a great deal of waste, now making some of the best farms in that district. Next after Mr. Rose of Dingwall, the principal instrument in clearing Strathconon was the late James Gillanders of Highfield, already so well known to the reader in connection with the evictions at Glencalvie and elsewhere.

The Strathconon evictions are worthy of note for the forcible illustration they furnish of how, by these arbitrary and unexpected removals, hardships and ruin have frequently been brought on families and communities who were at the time in comfortable circumstances. At one time, and previous to the earlier evictions, perhaps no glen of its size in the Highlands had a larger population than Strathconon. The club farm system, once so common in the North, seems to have been peculiarly successful here. Hence, a large proportion of the people were well to do but, when suddenly called upon to give up their hill pasture and afterwards their arable land, and in the absence of other suitable places to settle, the means they had very soon disappeared and the trials and difficulties of new conditions had to be encountered. As a rule, in most of these Highland evictions, the evicted were lost sight of, having either emigrated to foreign lands or become absorbed in the ever-increasing unemployed population of the large towns. In the case of Strathconon, it was different. With regard to those evicted families who were allowed to settle in the Black Isle, the excellent agricultural condition into which they brought their smallholdings is a standing refutation of the charge so often made against the Highland people, that they are lazy and incapable of properly cultivating the land.

The Black Isle

Respecting the estates of Drynie and Kilcoy, a correspondent, who says, 'I well remember my excessive grief when my father had to leave the farm which his forefathers had farmed for five generations,' writes:

'All the tenants to the east of Drynie, as far as Craigiehow, were turned out, one by one, to make room for one large tenant, Mr. Robertson, who had no less than four centres for stackyards. A most prosperous tenantry were turned out to make room for him and what is the end of it all! Mr. Robertson has come to grief as a farmer and now holds a very humble position in the town of Inverness. Drumderfit used to be occupied by fifteen or sixteen tenants who were gradually evicted during the last fifty years. Balnakyle was tenanted by five very comfortable and respectable farmers, four of whom were turned out within the last thirty years; Balnaguie was occupied by three; Torr by six; and Croft-cruive by five; the once famous names of Drum-na-marg and Moreton are now extinct, as well as the old tenantry whose forefathers farmed these places for generations. The present farm of Kilcoy includes a number of holdings whose tenants were evicted to make room for one large farmer and this is equally true of many others in the district.

The Island of Lewis

No one was evicted from the Island of Lewis, in the strict sense of the term, but 2,231 souls had to leave it between 1851 and 1863. To pay their passage money and their inland railway fares on arrival, and to provide them with clothing and other furnishings, the late Sir James Matheson paid a sum of £11,855. In spite of all this expenditure, many of these poor people would have died from starvation on their arrival without the good offices of friends in Canada.

In 1841, before Mr. Matheson bought it, a cargo of emigrants from Lewis arrived at Quebec late in the autumn, accompanied by a Rev. Mr. Maclean, sent to minister to their spiritual wants. It appears that no provision had been made for the more pressing demands of a severe Canadian winter and, were it not for the Saint Andrew's Society of Montreal, every soul of them would have been starved to death that winter in a strange land. The necessities of the case, and how this patriotic Society saved their countrymen from a horrid death will be seen on perusal of the following minutes, extracted from the books of the Society, during the writer's recent tour in Canada: 'A special meeting of the office-bearers was summoned on the 20th September, 1841, to take into consideration an application made by Mr. Morris, President of the Emigration Association of the district of St. Francis, for some pecuniary aid to a body of 229 destitute emigrants who had recently arrived from the Island of Lewis (Scotland), and who were then supported chiefly by the contributions of the charitable inhabitants of the town of Sherbrooke and its neighbourhood. Mr. Morris' letter intimated that, unless other assistance was received, it would be impossible for these emigrants to outlive the winter, as they were in a state of utter destitution. The meeting decided that the Constitution of the Society prohibited them from applying its funds to an object like the one presented – it did not appear to authorize the granting of relief from its funds except to cases of destitution in the city but, as this case appeared of an urgent nature, and one particularly calling for assistance, Messrs. Hew Ramsay and Neil McIntosh were appointed to collect subscriptions on behalf of the emigrants. This committee acquitted itself with great diligence and success, having collected the handsome sum of £234 14s. 6d., all of which was, at different times, remitted to Mr. Morris and expended by him in this charity. Letters were received from Mr. Morris, expressing the gratitude of the emigrants for this large and timely aid, which was principally the means of keeping them from starvation.' The whole of these emigrants are now in easy circumstances.

The idea of sending out a minister and nothing else, in such circumstances makes one shudder to think of the uses which are sometimes made of the clergy and how, in such cases, the Gospel they are supposed not only to preach but to practise is only in many instances caricatured. The provisions sent by the Society had to be forwarded to where these starving emigrants were, a distance of eighty miles from Sherbrooke, on sledges, through a dense, trackless forest. The descendants of these people now form a happy and prosperous community at Lingwick and Winslow.

The Leckmelm Evictions

The small property of Leckmelm in the Parish of Lochbroom changed hands in 1879, Mr. A. C. Pirie, paper manufacturer, Aberdeen, having purchased it for £19,000 from Colonel Davidson, now of Tulloch. No sooner did it come into Mr. Pirie's possession than a notice, dated 2nd November, 1879, in the following terms, was issued to all the tenants:

'I am instructed by Mr. Pirie, proprietor of Leckmelm, to give you notice that the present arrangements by which you hold the cottage, byre and other buildings, together with lands on that estate, will cease from and after the term of Martinmas, 1880 and, further, I am instructed to intimate to you that at the said term of Martinmas, 1880, Mr. Pirie intends taking the whole arable and pasture lands, but that he wishes to make arrangements whereby you may continue tenant of the cottage upon terms and conditions yet to be settled upon. I have further to inform you that unless you and the other tenants at once prevent your sheep and other stock from grazing or trespassing upon the enclosures and hill, and other lands now in the occupation or possession of the said Mr. Pirie, he will not, upon any conditions, permit you to remain in the cottage you now occupy, after the said term of Martinmas, 1880, but will clear all off the estate, and take down the cottages.'

This notice affected twenty-three families, numbering above one hundred souls. Sixteen tenants paid between them a rent of £96 10s., ranging from £3 to £12 each per annum. The stock allowed them was seventy-two head of cattle, eight horses and three hundred and twenty sheep. The arable portion of Leckmelm was about the best tilled and most productive land in possession of any crofters in the parish. It could all be worked with the plough, now a very uncommon thing in the Highlands for, almost invariably, land of that class is in the hands of the proprietors themselves, when not let to sheep farmers or sportsmen. At Martinmas, 1880, he took every inch of land into his own hands and thus, by one cruel stroke, reduced a comfortable tenantry from comparative affluence and independence to the position of mere cottars and day labourers, absolutely dependent for subsistence on his will and the likes or dislikes of his subordinates. With the exception of one, all the tenants who remained are still permitted to live in their old cottages but they are not permitted to keep a living thing about them, not even a hen. They are existing in a state of abject dependence on Mr. Pirie's will and that of his servants and in a constant state of terror that they will be turned out of their cottages. As regards work and the necessaries of life, they have been reduced to that of common navvies. In place of milk, butter and cheese in fair abundance, they have now to be satisfied with sugar, treacle or whatever else they can buy, to their porridge and potatoes, and their supply of meat, grown and fed up to now by themselves, is gone for ever. Two, a man and his wife, if not more, have since been provided for by the parochial authorities, and, no doubt, that will be the fate of many more of this once-thriving and contented people.

A protest against Mr. Pirie's conduct was raised at the time and the advantage which he had taken of his position was universally condemned by the press (excepting *The Scotsman*) and by the general public voice of the country but, conscious that the law, made by the landlords in their own interests, was on his side, he relentlessly and persistently carried out his cruel purpose to the bitter end and evicted from their lands and hill grazings every soul upon his property. In the meantime, he allowed them to remain in their cottages, with the exception of Donald Munro, to whose case reference will be made hereafter, and two other persons whose houses were pulled down and they themselves evicted.

91

When the notices of removal were received, the Rev. John MacMillan, Free Church minister of the parish, called public attention to Mr. Pirie's proceedings in the Northern newspapers, and soon the eye of the whole country was directed to this modern evictor – a man, in other respects, reputed to be kind to those under him in his business of paper manufacturing in Aberdeen. People, in their simplicity, for years back, thought that evictions on such a large scale, in the face of a more enlightened public opinion, had become mere unpleasant recollections of a barbarous past, forgetting that the same laws which permitted the Clearances of Sutherland and other portions of the Scottish Highlands during the first half of the present century were still in force, ready to be applied by any tyrant who had the courage, for personal ends, to outrage the more advanced and humane public opinion of the present generation.

The noble conduct of the Rev. Mr. MacMillan in connection with those evictions deserves equal commemoration to that earned by his prototype in Sutherland, the Rev. Mr. Sage, during the infamous Clearances in that county. At the urgent request of many friends of the Highland crofters resident in Inverness, Mr. MacMillan agreed to lay the case of his evicted parishioners before the public. Early in December, 1880, he delivered an address in Inverness to one of the largest and most enthusiastic meetings which has ever been held in that town, and we cannot do better here than quote at considerable length from his instructive, eloquent and rousing appeal on that occasion. Though his remarks do not seem to have influenced Mr. Pirie's conduct or to have benefited his unfortunate subjects, the Inverness meeting was the real beginning in earnest of the subsequent movement throughout the Highlands in favour of Land Reform, and the curtailment of landlord power over their unfortunate tenants. Mr. Pirie can thus claim to have done our poorer countrymen no small amount of good, though probably quite contrary to his intentions, by his cruel and high-handed conduct in dealing with the ancient tenants of Leckmelm. He has set the heather on fire, and it is likely to continue burning until such proceedings as those for which he is responsible at Leckmelm will be finally made impossible in Scotland.

Mr. MacMillan, after informing his audience that Mr. Pirie 'is now in a fair way of reaching a notoriety which he little dreamt of when he became owner of the Leckmelm estate', proceeds to tell how the harsh proceedings were gone about, and says:

'As the public are aware, Mr. Pirie's first step after becoming owner of the estate, was to inform the tenantry, by the hands of Mr. Manners, C.E., Inverness, that, at Martinmas following, they were to deliver their arable land and stock, consisting of sheep and cattle, into his hands, but that some of them, on conditions yet to be revealed, and on showing entire submission to the new *regime* of things and withal a good certificate of character from his factotum, William Gould, might remain in their cottages to act as serfs on his farm. On this conditional promise they were to live in the best of hope for the future, and all at the mercy of the absolute master of the situation, with a *summum jus* at his back to enable him to effect all the purposes of his heart. As a prologue to the drama which was to follow, and to give a sample of what they might expect in the sequel, two acts were presented, or, properly speaking, one act in two parts. These were to prepare them for what was to come, reminding us of what we read somewhere in our youth, of a husband who, on marrying his fair spouse, wished to teach her prompt obedience to all his commands, whatever their character. His first lesson in this direction was one assuredly calculated to strike terror into her tender breast. It was the shooting on the spot of the horse which drew his carriage or conveyance, on showing some slight restiveness. The second lesson was of a similar nature; we can easily imagine that his object was gained. Then, after coming home, he commanded his spouse to untie his boots and take them off, and to engage in the most servile acts. Of course, prompt obedience was given to all these commands and his end was gained. His wife was obedient to him to the last degree. Of the wisdom and propriety of such a procedure in a husband towards his lawful wife, I shall not here and now wait to enquire, but one thing is plain to us all: there was a species of earthly and carnal wisdom in it which was overshadowed by its cruelty.

'Now this illustrates exactly how Mr. Pirie acted towards the people of Leckmelm. To strike terror into their hearts, first of all, two houses were pulled down, I might say about the ears of their respective occupants, without any warning whatever, except a verbal one of the shortest kind. The first was a deaf pauper woman about middle life, living alone for years in a bothy of her own, apart from the other houses, beside a purling stream, where she had at all seasons pure water to drink, if her bread was at times somewhat scanty. After this most cruel eviction, no provision was made for the helpless woman but she was allowed to get shelter elsewhere as best she could. If any of you ever go the way of Leckmelm, you can see a gamekeeper's house, the gentry of our land, close to the side of Iseabal Bheag's bothy, and a dog kennel quite in its neighbourhood or, as I said in one of my letters, adorning it. This, then, is act the first of this drama. Act second comes next. Mrs. Campbell was a widow with two children; after the decease of her husband, she tried to support herself and them by serving in gentlemen's families as a servant. Whether she was all the time in Tulloch's family I cannot say but, at all events, it was from that family she returned to Leckmelm in failing health and on getting rather heavy for active service. Of course, her father had died since she had left, and the house in which he lived and died and in which, in all likelihood, he had reared his family and in which he was born and bred, was now tenantless. It was empty, the land attached to it being in the hands of another person. Here Widow Campbell settled for a while until something else would in kind Providence turn up. But, behold, during her sojourn from her native township, another king arose, who knew not Joseph, and the inexorable edict had gone forth to raze her habitation to the ground. Her house also was pulled down about her ears. This woman has since gone to America, the asylum of many a family evicted from hearth and home. Such tragedies as I have mentioned roused some of us to remonstrate with the actors engaged in them and, to the best of our ability, to expose their conduct and, furthermore, we have brought them to the bar of public judgment to pass their verdict, which I hope before all is over, will be one of condemnation and condign punishment.'

94

Having referred at some length to the worst classes of evictions throughout the Highlands in the past, and already described in this work, the reverend lecturer proceeded:

'But there is another way, a more gentle, politic and insinuating way at work which depopulates our country quite as effectually as the wholesale Clearances of which we have been speaking and against which we protest. There are many proprietors who get the name of being good and kind to their tenants and who cannot be charged with evicting any of them save for misbehaviour. who are, nevertheless, inch by inch secretly and stealthily laying waste the country and undermining the wellbeing of our people. I have some of these gentlemen before my mind at this moment. When they took possession of their estates, all promised fair and well but, by and by, the fatal blow was struck, to dispossess the people of their sheep. Mark that *first move* and resist it to the utmost. As long as tenants have a hold of the hill pasture by sheep, and especially if it be what we term a commonage or club farm, it is impossible to lay it waste in part. But, once you snap this tie asunder, you are henceforth at the mercy of the owner to do with you as he pleases. This then is how the business is transacted, and in the most businesslike fashion too. To be sure, none are to be forcibly evicted from their holdings: that would be highly unwise. It would bring public condemnation on the sacred heads of the evictors, which some of them could not face, for they have a name to sustain, and also because they are more susceptible to the failings common to humanity. They are moving, too, in the choicest circles of society. It would not do that their names should be figuring in every newspaper in the land, as cruel and oppressive landlords, or that the Rev. this and the Rev. that should excommunicate them from society and stigmatize them as tyrants and despots. But all are not so sensitive of name as this, as we see abundantly demonstrated, because they have none to lose. You might expose them upon a gibbet before the gaze of an assembled universe and they would hardly blush, "they are harder than the nether millstone". But the more sensitive do their work all the same and it is done in this fashion. When a tenant dies or removes otherwise, the order goes forth that his croft or lot is to be

95

laid waste. It is not given to a neighbouring tenant, except in some instances, nor to a stranger, to occupy it. In this inch-by-inch Clearance, the work of depopulation is effected in a few years, or in a generation at most, quite as effectually as by the more glaring and reprehensible method. This more secret and insinuating way of depopulating our native land should be as stoutly resisted as the more open and defiant one, for the result it produces is the same.'

Describing the character of the Highlanders, as shown by their conduct in our Highland regiments, and the impossibility of recruiting from them in future if harsh evictions are not stopped, the reverend gentleman continued:

'Let me give you words more eloquent than mine on this point, which will show the infatuation of our Government in allowing her bravest soldiers to be driven to foreign lands and to be crushed and oppressed by the tyrant's rod. After having asked, What have these people done against the State when they were so remorselessly driven from their native shores year by year in batches of thousands? What class have they wronged that they should suffer a penalty so dreadful? this writer gives the answer: They have done no wrong. Yearly they have sent forth their thousands from their glens to follow the battle flag of Britain wherever it flew. It was a Highland *rearlorn* hope that followed the broken wreck of Cumberland's army after the disastrous day at Fontenoy when more British soldiers lay dead upon the field than fell at Waterloo itself. It was another Highland regiment that scaled the rock-face over the St. Lawrence, and first formed a line in the September dawn on the level sward of Abraham. It was a Highland line that broke the power of the Maharatta hordes and gave Wellington his maiden victory at Assaye. Thirty-four battalions marched from these glens to fight in America, Germany and India before the 18th century had run its course and yet, while abroad over the earth, Highlanders were the first in assault and the last in retreat. Their lowly homes in far-away glens were being dragged down and the wail of women and the cry of children went out on the same breeze that bore upon its wings the scent of heather, the freshness of gorse blossom and the myriad sweets that made the lowly life of

Scotland's peasantry blest with health and happiness. These are crimes done in the dark hours of strife and amid the blaze of man's passions, which sometimes make the blood run cold as we read them but they are not so terrible in their red-handed vengeance as the cold malignity of a civilized law, which permits a brave and noble race to disappear by the operation of its legalized injustice. To convert the Highland glens into vast wastes untenanted by human beings; to drive forth to distant and inhospitable shores men whose forefathers had held their own among these hills, despite Roman legion, Saxon archer or Norman chivalry, men whose sons died freely for England's honour, through those wide dominions their bravery had won for her. Such was the work of laws formed in a cruel mockery of name by the Commons of England. Around 1808, the stream of Highland soldiery, which had been gradually ebbing, gave symptoms of running completely dry. Recruits for Highland regiments could not be obtained for the simple reason that the Highlands had been depopulated. Six regiments which, from the date of their foundation had worn the kilt and bonnet, were ordered to lay aside their distinctive uniform and henceforth became merged into the ordinary line corps. From the mainland the work of destruction passed rapidly to the isles. These remote resting-places of the Celt were quickly cleared. During the first ten years of the great war, Skye had given 4,000 of its sons to the army. It has been computed that 1,600 Skyemen stood in the ranks at Waterloo. Today in Skye, far as the eye can reach, nothing but a bare brown waste is to be seen, where still the mounds and ruined gables rise over the melancholy landscapes, sole vestiges of a soldier race for ever passed away.

'In January, 1882, news had reached Inverness that Murdo Munro, one of the most comfortable tenants on the Leckmelm property, had been turned out, with his wife and young family, in the snow; whereupon the writer started to enquire into the facts, and spent a whole day among the people. What he had seen proved to be as bad as any of the evictions of the past, except that it applied in this instance only to one family. Murdo Munro was too independent for the local managers and, to some extent, led the people in their opposition to Mr.

Pirie's proceedings: he was first persecuted and afterwards evicted in the most cruel fashion. Other reasons were afterwards given for the manner in which this poor man and his family were treated but it has been shown conclusively in a report published at the time that these reasons were an afterthought. From this report we shall quote a few extracts:

'So long as the laws of the land permit men like Mr. Pirie to drive from the soil without compensation the men who, by their labour and money, made their properties what they are, it must be admitted that he is acting within his legal rights, however much we may deplore the manner in which he has chosen to exercise them. We have to deal more with the system which allows him to act thus than with the special reasons which he considers sufficient to justify his proceedings. If his conduct in Leckmelm will, as I trust it may, hasten on a change in our land legislation, the hardships endured by the luckless people who had the misfortune to come under his unfeeling yoke and his ideas of moral right and wrong will be more than counterbalanced by the benefits which will ultimately accrue to the people at large. This is why I and, I believe, the public, take such an interest in this question of the evictions at Leckmelm.

'I have made the most careful and complete enquiry possible among Mr. Pirie's servants, the tenants, and the people of Ullapool. Mr. Pirie's local manager, after I had informed him of my object and put him on his guard as to the use which I might make of his answers, informed me that he never had any fault to find with Munro, that he always found him quite civil, and that he had nothing to say against him. The tenants, without exception, spoke of him as a good neighbour. The people of Ullapool, without exception, so far as I could discover, after enquiries from the leading men in every section of the community, speak well of him and condemn Mr. Pirie. Munro is universally spoken of as one of the best workmen in the whole parish and, by his industry and sobriety, he has been able to save a little money in Leckmelm, where he was able to keep a fairly good stock on his small farm, and worked steadily with a horse and cart. The stock handed over by him to Mr. Pirie consisted of one bull, two cows, one

98

stirk, one Highland pony and about forty sheep, which represented a considerable saving. Several of the other tenants had a similar stock and some of them had even more, all of which they had to dispense with under the new arrangements, and consequently lost the annual income in money and produce available therefrom. We all know that the sum received for this stock cannot last long and cannot be advantageously invested in anything else. The people must now live on their small capital, instead of what it produced, so long as it lasts, after which they are sure to be helpless, and many of them become chargeable to the parish.

'The system of petty tyranny which prevails at Leckmelm is scarcely credible. Contractors have been told not to employ Munro. For this I have the authority of some of the contractors themselves. Local employers of labour were requested not to employ any longer people who had gone to look on among the crowd while Munro's family, goods and furniture were being turned out. Letters were received by others complaining of the same thing from higher quarters and threatening ulterior consequences. Of all this I have the most complete evidence but, in the interests of those involved, I shall mention no names except in Court, where I challenge Mr. Pirie and his subordinates to the proof if they deny it.

'The extract in the action of removal was signed only on the 24th of January last in Dingwall. On the following day the charge is dated and two days after, on the 27th of January, the eviction is complete. When I visited the scene on Friday morning, I found a substantially built cottage and a stable at the end of it, unroofed to within three feet of the top on either side, and the whole surroundings a perfect scene of desolation; the thatch and part of the furniture, including portions of broken bedsteads, tubs, basins, teapots and various other articles, strewn outside. The cross-beams, couples and cabars were still there, a portion of the latter brought from Mr. Pirie's manager and paid for within the last three years. The Sheriff officers had placed a padlock on the door but I made my way to the inside of the house through one of the windows from which the frame and glass had been removed. I found that the house, before the partitions had been

99

removed, consisted of two good-sized rooms and a closet, with fire-place and chimney in each gable, the crook still hanging in one of them, the officer having apparently been unable to remove it after a considerable amount of wrenching. The kitchen window, containing eight panes of glass, was still whole, but the closet window, with four panes, had been smashed, while the one in the "ben" end of the house had been removed. The cottage, as crofters' houses go, must have been fairly comfortable. Indeed, the cottages in Leckmelm are altogether superior to the usual run of crofters' houses on the West Coast and the tenants are allowed to have been the most comfortable in all respects in the parish, before the land was taken from them. They are certainly not the poor, miserable creatures, badly housed, which Mr. Pirie and his friends led the public to believe within the last two years.

'The barn in which the wife and infant had to remain all night had the upper part of both gables blown out by the recent storm and the door was scarcely any protection from the weather. The potatoes, which had been thrown out in showers of snow, were still there, gathered and with a little earth put over them by the friendly neighbours.

'The mother and children wept piteously during the eviction and many of the neighbours, afraid to help or shelter them, were visibly affected to tears. The whole scene was such that, if Mr. Pirie could have seen it, I feel sure that he would never consent to be held responsible for another. His humanity would soon drive his stern ideas of legal right out of his head, and we would hear no more of evictions at Leckmelm.'

Those tenants who are still at Leckmelm are permitted to remain in their cottages as half-yearly tenants on payment of 12s. per annum, but liable to be removed at any moment that their absolute lord may take it into his head to evict them, or when they may give the slightest offence to any of his meanest subordinates.

The Lochcarron Evictions

The following account was written in April, 1882, after a most careful enquiry on the spot:

100

So much whitewash has been distributed in our Northern newspapers of late by 'Local Correspondents' in the interests of personal friends who are responsible for the Lochcarron evictions – the worst and most indefensible that have ever been attempted even in the Highlands – that we consider it a duty to state the facts. We are really sorry for those more immediately concerned but our friendly feeling for them otherwise cannot be allowed to come between us and our plain duty. A few days before the famous 'Battle of the Braes' on the Isle of Skye, we received information that summonses of ejectment were served on Mackenzie and Maclean, Lochcarron. The writer at once communicated with Mr. Dugald Stuart, the proprietor, intimating to him the statements received and asking if they were accurate and if he had anything to say in explanation. Mr. Stuart immediately replied, admitting the accuracy of the statements generally but maintaining that he had good and valid reasons for carrying out the evictions, which he expressed himself anxious to explain to us on the following day, while passing through Inverness on his way south. Unfortunately, his letter reached us too late and we were unable to see him. The only reason which he vouchsafed to give in his letter was to the following effect: was it at all likely that he, a Highlander, born and brought up in the Highlands, the son of a Highlander and married to a Highland lady, would be guilty of evicting any of his tenants without good cause? We replied that all these reasons could be urged by most of those who had in the past depopulated the country but, expressing a hope that, in his case, the facts stated by him would prove sufficient to restrain him from carrying out his determination to evict parents admittedly innocent of their sons' proceedings, even if those proceedings were unjustifiable. Early in April, 1882, we went to Lochcarron to make enquiries on the spot and the writer, on his return from Skye a few days later, reported as follows to the Highland Land Law Reform Association:

'Of all the cases of eviction which have hitherto come under my notice I never heard of any so utterly unjustifiable as those now in course of being carried out by Mr. D. Stuart in Lochcarron. The circumstances which led up to these evictions are as follows: in March,

1881, two young men, George Mackenzie and Donald Maclean, masons, entered into a contract with Mr. Stuart's ground officer for the erection of a sheep fank, and a dispute afterwards arose as to payment for the work. When the factor, Mr. Donald Macdonald, Tormore, was some time afterwards collecting the rents in the district, the contractors approached him and related their grievance against the ground officer, who, while the men were in the room, came in and addressed them in libellous and defamatory language, for which they have since obtained substantial damages and expenses, in all amounting to £22 13s. 8d., in the Sheriff Court of the County. I have a certified copy of the whole proceedings in Court in my possession and, without going into the merits, what I have just stated is the result, and Mr. Stuart and his ground officer became furious.

'The contractors are two single men who live with their parents, the latter being crofters on Mr. Stuart's property, and as the real offenders – if such can be called men who have stood up for and succeeded in establishing their rights and their characters in Court – could not be got at, Mr. Stuart issued summonses of ejection against their parents. The father of one of them strongly urged his son not to proceed against the ground officer, pointing out that an eviction might ensue and that it was better even to suffer in character and purse than run the risk of eviction from his holding at the age of eighty. We have all heard of the doctrine of visiting the sins of the parents upon the children, but it has been left for Mr. Dugald Stuart of Lochcarron and his ground officer, in the present generation to reverse all this, and to punish the unoffending parents for proceedings on the part of their children which the Sheriff of the County and all unprejudiced people who know the facts consider fully justifiable.

'Now, after careful enquiry among the men's neighbours and in the village of Lochcarron, nothing can be said against either of them. Their characters are in every respect above suspicion. The ground officer, whom I have seen, admits all this, and does not pretend that the eviction is for any other reason than the conduct of the young men in prosecuting and succeeding against himself in the Sheriff Court for defamation of character. Maclean paid rent for his present

102

holding for the last sixty years, and never failed to pay it on the appointed day. His father, grandfather and great-grandfather occupied the same place and so did their ancestors before them. Indeed, his grandfather held one-half of the township, now occupied by more than a hundred people. The old man is in his eighty-first year and bed-ridden since the middle of January last, when he had a paralytic stroke from which he will never recover. It was most pitiable to see the aged and frail human wreck as I saw him that day, and to have heard him talking of the cruelty and hard-heartedness of those who took advantage of the law to push him out of the home which he has occupied so long while he is on the brink of death. I quite agreed with him and I have no hesitation in saying that, if Mr. Stuart and his ground officer only called to see the miserable old man, their hearts, however adamantine, would melt and they would at once declare that he would be allowed to end his days and die in peace under the roof which for generations had sheltered his family. The wife is over seventy years of age, and the frail old couple have no one to succour them but the son who has been the cause, by defending his own character, of their present misfortunes. Whatever Mr. Stuart and his ground officer may do, the old man will not and cannot be evicted until he is carried to the churchyard and it would be far more gracious on their part to allow the old man to die in peace.

'Mackenzie has paid rent for over forty years and his ancestors have done so for several generations before him. He is nearly sixty years of age and is highly popular among his neighbours, all of whom are intensely grieved at Mr. Stuart's cruel and hard-hearted conduct towards him and Maclean and they still hope that he will not proceed to extremities.

'The whole case is a lamentable abuse of the existing law and such as will do more to secure its abolition when the facts are fully known than all the other cases of eviction which have taken place in the Highlands during the present generation. There is no pretence that the case is anything else than a gross and cruel piece of retaliation against the innocent parents for conduct on the part of their sons, which must have been very aggravating to this proprietor and his

103

ground officer, who appear to think themselves fully justified in perpetuating such acts of grossest cruelty and injustice.'

This report was slightly noticed at the time in the local and Glasgow newspapers and attention was thus directed to Mr. Stuart's proceedings. His whole conduct appeared so tyrannical that most people expected him to relent before the day of eviction arrived. But not so; a Sheriff officer and his assistants from Dingwall duly arrived, and proceeded to turn Mackenzie's furniture out of his house. People congregated from all parts of the district, some of them coming more than twenty miles. The Sheriff officer sent for the Lochcarron policemen to aid him but the law which permitted such unmitigated cruelty and oppression was challenged; the Sheriff officers were deforced and the furniture returned to the house by the sympathizing crowd. What was to be done next? The Procurator Fiscal for the county was Mr. Stuart's law agent in carrying out the evictions. How could he criminally prosecute for deforcement in these circumstances? The Crown authorities found themselves in a dilemma and, through the tyranny of the proprietor on the one hand and the interference of the Procurator-Fiscal in civil business which has ended in public disturbance and deforcement of the Sheriff officers on the other, the Crown authorities found themselves helpless to vindicate the law. This is a pity, for all right-thinking people have almost as little sympathy for law breakers, even when that law is unjust and cruel, as they have for those cruel landlords who, like Mr. Stuart of Lochcarron, bring the law and their own order into disrepute by the oppressive application of it against innocent people. The proper remedy is to have the law abolished, not to break it and, to bring this about, such conduct as that of Mr. Stuart and his ground officer is more potent than all the Land Leagues and Reform Associations in the United Kingdom.

Mr. William Mackenzie of the *Aberdeen Free Press,* who was on the ground, writes, next morning, after the deforcement of the Sheriff officers:

'During the encounter the local police constable drew his baton but he was peremptorily ordered to lay it down and he did so. The officers then gave up the contest and left the place about three in the morning. Yesterday before they left and in the course of the evening, they were offered refreshments, but these they declined. The people are this evening in possession as before.

'When every article was restored to its place, the song and the dance were resumed, the native drink was freely quaffed – for freedom an' whisky gang the gither – the steam was kept up throughout the greater part of yesterday and Mackenzie's mantelpiece today is adorned with a long tier of empty bottles, standing there as monuments to the eventful night of the 29th–30th May, 1882.

> A chuirm sgaolite chualas an ceòl
> Ard-shòlas an talla nan treun!

'While these things were going on in the quiet township of Slumbay, the Fiery Cross appears to have been despatched over the neighbouring parishes; and from Kintail, Lochalsh, Applecross and even Gairloch, the Highlanders began to gather yesterday with the view of helping the Slumbay men, if occasion should arise. Few of these reached Slumbay, but they were in small detachments in the neighbourhood ready at any moment to come to the rescue on the appearance of any hostile force. After all the trains had come and gone for the day, and as neither policemen nor Sheriff officers had appeared on the scene, these different groups retired to their respective places of abode. The Slumbay men, too, resolved to suspend their festivities. A procession was formed and, headed by the piper, they marched triumphantly through Slumbay and Jeantown and escorted some of the strangers on their way to their homes, returning to Slumbay in the course of the night.'

As a contrast to Mr. Stuart's conduct, we are glad to record the noble action of Mr. C. J. Murray, M.P. for Hastings, who has, fortunately for the oppressed tenants on the Lochcarron property, just purchased the estate. He has made it a condition that Maclean and Makenzie shall be allowed to remain and a further public scandal has thus been avoided.

The factor on the estate, Mr. Donald Macdonald of Tormore strongly urged upon Mr Stuart not to evict these people and his own wife also implored and begged of him not to carry out his cruel and vindictive purpose. Where these agencies failed, it is gratifying to find that Mr. Murray has succeeded; and all parties – landlords and tenants – throughout the Highlands are to be congratulated on the result.

CHAPTER III

*J*NVERNESS-SHIRE

Glengarry

Glengarry was peopled down to the end of last century with a fine race of men. In 1745, six hundred stalwart vassals followed the chief of Glengarry to the battle of Culloden. Some few years later, they became so disgusted with the return made by their chief that many of them emigrated to the United States, though they were almost all in comfortable circumstances. In spite of this semi–voluntary exodus, Major John Macdonell of Lochgarry was able in 1777 to raise a fine regiment – the 76th, or Macdonald, Highlanders – numbering 1,086 men, 750 of whom were Highlanders, mainly from the Glengarry property. In 1794, Alexander Macdonnell of Glengarry raised a Fencible regiment, described as 'a handsome body of men', of whom half were enlisted on the same estate. On being disbanded in 1802, these men were again so shabbily treated that they followed the example of the men of the Forty-five and emigrated in a body with their families to Canada, taking two Gaelic-speaking ministers along with them to their new home. They afterwards distinguished themselves as part of the 'Glengarry Fencibles' of Canada, in defence of their adopted country, calling their settlement there after their native glen in Scotland. The chiefs of Glengarry drove away their people, only to be themselves ousted soon after them.

The Glengarry property at one time covered an area of nearly 200 square miles and today, while many of their expatriated vassals are landed proprietors and in affluent circumstances in Canada, not an inch of the old possessions of the ancient and powerful family of

107

Glengarry remains to the descendants of those who caused the banishment of a people who, on many a well-fought field, shed their blood for their chief and country. In 1853, every inch of the ancient heritage was possessed by strangers, except Knoydart in the west, which has long ago become the property of one of the Bairds. At that time, young Glengarry was a minor, his mother, the widow of the late chief, being one of his trustees. She does not appear to have learned any lesson of wisdom from the past misfortunes of her house. Indeed, considering her limited power and possessions, she was comparatively the worst of them all.

The tenants of Knoydart, like all other Highlanders, had suffered severely during and after the potato famine in 1846 and 1847 and some of them got into arrears with a year's and some with two years' rent but they were fast clearing it off. Mrs. Macdonell and her factor decided to evict every crofter on her property to make room for sheep. In the spring of 1853, they were all served with summonses of removal, accompanied by a message that Sir John Macneil, chairman of the Board of Supervision, had agreed to convey them to Australia. Their feelings were not considered worthy of the slightest consideration. They were not even asked whether they would prefer to follow their countrymen to America and Canada. They were to be treated as if they were nothing better than slaves. The people, however, had no alternative but to accept any offer made to them. They could not get an inch of land on any of the neighbouring estates and anyone who would give them a night's shelter was threatened with eviction.

It was afterwards found inconvenient to transport them to Australia. The poor creatures were then told that they would be taken to North America and that a ship would be at Isle Ornsay on the Isle of Skye in a few days to receive them and that they must go on board. The *Sillery* soon arrived. Mrs. Macdonell and her factor came all the way from Edinburgh to see the people hounded across in boats and put on board this ship whether they wanted to go or not. An eyewitness who described the proceedings at the time, whom we met a few years ago in Nova Scotia, characterizes the scene as heart-rending. 'The wail of the poor women and children as they were torn away from their homes would have melted a heart of stone.' Some few families, principally cottars, refused to go, in spite of every influence brought to bear upon them and the treatment they afterwards received was cruel beyond belief. The houses, not only of those who went but of those who remained, were burned and levelled to the ground. The strath was dotted all over with black spots showing where once stood their homes. The scarred half-burned wood was strewn about in every direction. Stooks of corn and plots of unlifted potatoes could be seen on all sides but man was gone. Those who refused to go aboard the *Sillery* were in hiding among the rocks and caves while their friends were packed off like so many slaves.

No mercy was shown to those who refused to emigrate; their few articles of furniture were thrown out of their houses after them – beds, chairs, tables, pots, stoneware, clothing, in many cases, rolling down the hill. What took years to erect and collect was destroyed and scattered in a few minutes. 'From house to house, from hut to hut and from barn to barn, the factor and his menials proceeded, carrying on the work of demolition, until there was scarcely a human habitation left standing in the district. Able-bodied men who, if the matter would rest with a mere trial of physical force, would have bound the factor and his party hand and foot and sent them out of the district, stood aside as dumb spectators. Women wrung their hands and cried aloud, children ran to and fro, dreadfully frightened and, while all this demolition and destruction was going on, no opposition was offered by the inhabitants, no hand was lifted, no stone cast, no angry word spoken.' The few huts left undemolished were occupied by the paupers but, before the factor left for the South, even they were warned not to give any shelter to the evicted, or their huts would assuredly meet with the same fate. Eleven families, numbering in all over sixty persons, mostly old and decrepit men and women and helpless children, were exposed that night, and many of them long afterwards, to the cold air, without shelter of any description beyond what little they were able to save out of the wreck of their burned dwellings.

An account of the cruelties perpetrated on the poor Highlanders of Knoydart may, perhaps, serve a good purpose. It may convince the evil-doer that his work shall not be forgotten, and any who may be disposed to follow the example of past evictors may hesitate before they go on to immortalize themselves in such a hateful manner.

John Macdugald, aged about fifty, with a wife and family, was a cottar and earned his subsistence chiefly by fishing. He was in bad health and two of his sons were in hospital in Elgin suffering from smallpox when the *Sillery* was sent to convey the Knoydart people to Canada. He refused to go because of the state of his health and his boys being away in hospital. The factor and the officers arrived, turned Macdugald and his family adrift, put their bits of furniture out on the field and, in a few minutes, levelled their house to the ground. The whole family had now no shelter but the broad canopy of heaven. The mother and the youngest of the children could not sleep owing to the cold and the father, on account of his sickness, kept wandering about all night near where his helpless family lay. After the factor and the officers left the district, Macdugald and his wife went back to the ruins of their house, collected some of the stones and turf into something like walls, threw a few cabars across, covered them over with blankets, old sails and turf and then, with their children, crept underneath, trusting that they would be allowed to take shelter under this temporary covering. But alas, they were doomed to bitter disappointment. Less than a week later, the local manager, with a posse of officers and menials, crossed the country and destroyed every hut or shelter erected by the evicted peasantry. Macdugald was at this time away from Knoydart; his wife was at Inverie, six miles away, seeing a sick relative; the oldest children were working at the shore; and in the hut, when the manager came with the 'levellers', he found none of the family except Lucy and Jane, the two youngest. The moment they saw the officers, they screamed and fled for their lives. The demolition of the shelter was easily accomplished in two or three minutes and then the officers and menials of the manager amused themselves by seizing hold of chairs, stools, tables, spinning wheels or any other light articles by throwing them a considerable distance from the hut. Lucy and Jane walked in the direction of Inverie, hoping to meet their mother. They had not gone far when they missed the footpath and lost their way. Meanwhile the mother returned from Inverie and found the hut razed to the ground, her furniture scattered far and near, her bedclothes lying under turf, clay, and debris and her children gone! The other children returned from the shore and they too stood aside, horrified at the sudden destruction of their humble refuge and at the absence of their two little sisters. At first they thought they were under the ruins and, creeping down on their knees, they carefully removed every turf and stone but found nothing except a few broken dishes. A search began. The mother, brother and sisters set off in opposite directions, searching every place and calling their names but they found no trace of them. Night was now approaching and with it all hopes of finding them till next day were fast dying away. The mother was now returning as darkness was falling, and still she had about three miles to travel. She made for the footpath and looked round every bush, rock and hillock, hoping to find them. Sometimes she imagined that she saw her two girls some distance in front of her but it was an illusion caused by bushes about their size. The moon now emerged from behind a cloud and spread its light on the path and surrounding district. A sharp frost set in and ice began to form on the little pools. Passing near a rock and some bushes, where the children of the tenants used to meet when herding the cattle, she felt as if something beckoned her to search there. She found her two little children fast asleep, beside a favourite bush. They told their mother that, when they saw the officers, they crept out and ran in the direction of Inverie to tell her. They missed the footpath, then wandered about crying and finally somehow found their favourite herding ground, where, exhausted, they fell asleep. The mother took the young one on her back, sent the other on before her, and soon joined her other children near the ruins of their old dwelling. They put a few sticks up to an old fence, placed a blanket over it, and slept on the bare ground that night. Macdugald returned from his distant journey, found his family shelterless and again set about erecting some refuge for them from the wreck of the old buildings. Again, however, the local manager appeared with levellers, turned them all adrift and in a

111

few moments destroyed the shelter. This continued for a week or two until Macdugald's health became serious, and then a neighbouring farmer gave him and his family temporary shelter in an outhouse. For this act of disinterested humanity he received most improper and threatening letters from the managers on the estate of Knoydart. It is very likely that in consequence of this interference Macdugald is again taking shelter among the rocks or amid the wreck of his former residence.

John Mackinnon, a cottar, aged forty-four, with a wife and six children, had his house pulled down and he and his family, for the first night or two, had to burrow among the rocks near the shore. When he thought that the factor and his party had left the district, he emerged from the rocks, surveyed the ruins of his former home and saw his furniture and belongings exposed to the elements and now almost worthless. The demolition was so complete that it was impossible to make any use of the ruins of the old house. The ruins of an old chapel, however, were near at hand and parts of the walls were still standing. Mackinnon took his family there and, having swept away some rubbish and removed some grass and nettles, they placed a few poles up to one of the walls and spread some sails and blankets across. They brought in some hay, and laid it in a corner for a bed, stuck a piece of iron into the wall in another corner, on which they placed a crook, then kindled a fire. They put a pot on the fire, and boiled some potatoes and, when these and a few fish roasted on the embers were ready, Mackinnon and his family had their first proper meal since the destruction of their house.

Mackinnon is a tall man, but poor and unhealthy looking. His wife is a poor weak woman, worn down by disease and difficulty. The boys, Ronald and Archibald, are lying in their makeshift bed of hay on the ground, suffering from rheumatism and cholic. The other children are apparently healthy enough as yet, but very ragged. There is no door to their wretched abode. Mackinnon's wife was pregnant when she was turned out of her house among the rocks. Four days later she gave birth prematurely and this, and her exposure to the elements without shelter or nutritious diet, has brought on consumption, from which she will not recover.

There was something very solemn indeed in this scene. One would think that, as Mackinnon took refuge amid the ruins of this most singular, sanctified place, he would be left alone and no longer be molested by man. But alas, that was not to be. The manager of Knoydart and his minions appeared and invaded this helpless family within the walls of the sanctuary. They pulled down the sticks and sails set up within its ruins, put Mackinnon's wife and children out on the cold shore, threw his tables, stools, chairs, etc., over the walls, burned the hay on which they slept, put out the fire and then left the district. Four times have these officers broken in upon poor Mackinnon in this way, destroying his shelter and setting his family adrift on the cold coast of Knoydart. When I looked in upon these creatures last week, I found them in utter dread, having just learned that the officers would appear next day to destroy the huts again. The children looked at me as if I were a wolf; they crept behind their father and stared wildly, fearing I was a law officer. The sight was most painful. The very idea that, in Christian Scotland in the nineteenth century, these children should be subjected to such gross treatment reflects strongly upon our humanity and civilization. Had there been famine or pestilence or war, I could understand it and account for it, but suffering to gratify the ambition of some unfeeling spectator cannot be justified and deserves the condemnation of every Christian man. Had Mackinnon been in arrears of rent, which he was not, even this would not justify the inhuman conduct towards himself and his family. No words can describe the condition of this poor family.

Consider now the pitiful case of Elizabeth Gillies, a widow, aged sixty years. Neither age, sex nor circumstance saved this poor creature from the most wanton and cruel aggression. Her house was on the brow of a hill, near a stream that formed the boundary between a large sheep farm and the lands of the tenants of Knoydart. Widow Gillies was warned to quit, like the rest of the tenants, and was offered a passage first to Australia and then to Canada, but she refused to go, saying she could do nothing in Canada. The widow, however, made no promises, and the factor went away. She had a young daughter staying with her but, before the vessel that was to convey the Knoydart

113

people away arrived at Isle Ornsay, this young girl died, and poor Widow Gillies was left alone. When the time for pulling down the houses arrived, it was hoped that some mercy would have been shown to this poor, bereaved widow, but there was none. Widow Gillies was sitting inside her house when the factor and officers arrived. They ordered her to remove herself and effects instantly, as they were to pull down the house! She refused. Two men then took hold of her and tried to pull her out by force but she sat down beside the fire and would not move an inch. One of the assistants threw water on the fire and extinguished it and then joined the other two in forcibly removing the poor widow from the house. At first she struggled hard, seized hold of every post or stone within her reach, taking a death grasp of each to keep possession. But the officers were too many and too cruel for her. They struck her over the fingers, making her let go her hold, and then all she could do was to weep and cry out murder! She was ultimately pushed out of the door and crept on her hands and feet to a wall, exhausted from her struggle. When the men had got her outside, the work of destruction immediately commenced. Stools, chairs, tables, cupboard, spinning wheel, bed, blankets, straw, dishes, pots and chest were thrown out into the gutter. They broke down the partitions, took down the crook from over the fireplace, destroyed the hen roosts and beat the hens out through the broad vent in the roof of the house; then they set to work on the walls outside with picks and iron levers. They pulled down the thatch, cut the couples and in a few minutes the walls fell out, while the roof fell in with a dismal crash!

When the factor and his party were done with this house, they proceeded to another district, pulling down and destroying homes as they went along. Night fell and the poor helpless widow sat alone and cheerless. Allan Macdonald, a cottar, whose house was also pulled down, ran across the hill to see how she had been treated and found her moaning beside the wall. He led her to where his own children had taken shelter, treated her kindly and did all he could to comfort her under the circumstances.

When I visited Knoydart, I found the poor widow at work repair-

114

ing her shed, and such a shed, and such a dwelling I never before witnessed. She spoke remarkably well, and appeared to be a very sensible woman. She said it was indeed most ungrateful on the part of the representatives of Glengarry to have treated her so cruelly, that her predecessors were, from time immemorial, on the Glengarry estates, that many of them died fighting for the old chieftains and that they had always been true and faithful subjects.

Why did she refuse to go to Canada?

'For a very good reason,' she said, 'I am now old and not able to clear a way in the forests of Canada; besides, I am unfit for service; further, I am averse to leave my native country and, rather than leave it, I would much prefer that my grave was opened beside my dear daughter, although I should be buried alive!'

I left her in this miserable shed which she occupied and I doubt if there is another human residence like it in Europe. The wigwam of the wild Indian and the cave of the Greenlander are palaces by comparison and even the meanest dog-kennel in England would be a thousand times better as a place of residence. If this poor Highland woman can survive winter in this abode, it will be a miracle. The factor has issued a *ukase,* which aggravates all these cases of eviction with peculiar hardship; he has warned all and sundry on the Knoydart estates from receiving or entertaining the evicted peasantry into their houses under pain of removal.

Allan Macdonald, aged fifty-four, a widower with four children, was similarly treated. When His late Majesty George IV visited Scotland in 1823 and, when Highland lairds sent up to Edinburgh specimens of the bone and sinew – human produce – of their properties, old Glengarry took care to give Allan Macdonald a polite invitation to this 'Royal exhibition'. Alas, how matters have so sadly changed. Within the last thirty years, *man* has fallen off dreadfully in the estimation of Highland proprietors. Commercially speaking, Allan Macdonald has now no value at all. Had he been a roe, a deer, a sheep or a bullock, a Highland laird in speculating could estimate his 'real' worth to within a few shillings, but Allan is *only* a man. Then his children; they are of no value to the sportsman. They cannot be shot

115

at like hares, blackcocks or grouse, nor yet can they be sent south as game to feed the London market.

Another case is that of Archibald Macisaac, crofter, aged sixty-six, wife, fifty-four, and family of ten children.

Archibald's house, byre, barn and stable were levelled to the ground. The furniture of the house was thrown down the hill and a general destruction commenced. The roof, fixtures and woodwork were smashed to pieces, the walls razed to the very foundation and all that was left for poor Archibald to look upon was a black dismal wreck. Twelve people were thus deprived of their home in less than half-an-hour. It was illegal to have destroyed the barn, for, according to the law of Scotland, the outgoing or removing tenant is entitled to the use of the barn until his crops are disposed of. But in a remote spot like Knoydart the laws that concern them and define their rights are unknown to them.

Archibald had now to make do as best he could. No aid could be expected from the factor. He gathered his children beside an old fence when the destruction of his home was accomplished and spoke to them about the position in which they were placed, saying they must ask God to guide them. His wife and children wept but the old man said, 'Neither weeping nor reflection is of use now; we must prepare some shelter.' The children collected some logs and turf and, in the hollow between two ditches, the old man constructed a rude shelter for the night and kindled a fire. The family gathered and they engaged in worship and sang psalms together. Next morning they examined the ruins, picked up some broken pieces of furniture, dishes, etc., and then made another addition to their shelter in the ditch. Matters went on this way for about a week, when the local manager and his men came down upon them and, after much abuse for daring to take shelter on the lands of Knoydart, they destroyed the shelter and put old Archy and his people again out on the hill.

I found Archibald and his numerous family still at Knoydart, in a shelter beside the old ditch. It was a wretched residence: a feal, or turf erection, about three feet high, four feet broad and five feet long, was at the end of the shelter and this formed the sleeping place of the mother and her five daughters! They creep in and out on their knees and their bed is just a layer of hay on the cold earth of the ditch! There is monstrous cruelty in this treatment of British females and the laws that sanction or tolerate such flagrant and gross abuses are a disgrace to the Statute book and to the country that permits it. Macisaac and his family are, by all accounts, decent, respectable and well-behaved people. Is it not a monstrous injustice to treat them worse than slaves because they refuse to allow themselves to be packed off to the Colonies like so many bales of manufactured goods?

Again:

Donald Maceachan, a cottar at Arar, married with five children. This poor man, his wife and children survived twenty-three nights without any shelter but the broad and blue heavens. They kindled a fire, prepared their food beside a rock and then slept in the open air. Just imagine the condition of this poor mother, Donald's wife, nursing a delicate child and subjected to merciless wind and rain during a long October night. One of these melancholy nights, the blankets that covered them were frozen and white with frost.

The next case is as follows:

Charles Macdonald, aged seventy, a widower, having no family. This poor man was also 'keeled' for the Colonies, and, as he refused to go, his house was levelled to the ground. What on earth could old Charles do in America? Was there any mercy or humanity in offering him a free passage across the Atlantic? In England, Charles would have been considered an object of parochial protection and relief but in Scotland no such relief is afforded except to 'sick folks' and tender infants. There can be no question, however, that the factor looked forward to the period when Charles would become chargeable as a pauper and, acting as a 'prudent man', he resolved to get quit of him at once. Three or four pounds would send the old man across the Atlantic but, if he remained in Knoydart, it would likely take four or five pounds to keep him each year that he lived. When the factor and his party arrived at Charles's door, they knocked and demanded admission and the factor ordered the old man to quit. Taking up his plaid and staff and adjusting his blue bonnet, he walked out, merely remarking to the factor that the man who could turn out an old, inoffensive Highlander of seventy from such a place and at such a season, could do a great deal more if the laws of the country permitted him. Charles took to the rocks and from that day he has never gone near his old habitation. He has neither house nor home, but receives occasional supplies of food from his evicted neighbours *and he sleeps on the hill!* Poor old man, who would not pity him, who would not share with him a crust or a covering?

Alexander Macdonald, aged forty, with four children, had his house pulled down. His wife was pregnant; still the levellers thrust her out and then put the children out after her. The husband argued and protested but it was all in vain for, in a few minutes, all he had for his once-comfortable home was a lot of rubbish, blackened rafters, and heaps of stones. The levellers laughed at his protests and, when their work was over, moved away, leaving him to find refuge the best way he could. Alexander had, like the rest of his evicted brethren, to burrow among the rocks and in caves until he put up a temporary shelter amid the wreck of his old habitation, from which he was repeatedly driven away. For three days, Alexander Macdonald's wife lay sick beside a bush, where, owing to terror and exposure to cold, she had a miscarriage. She was then removed to the shelter of the walls of her former house and, for three days, she seemed likely to die. These are facts which cannot be contradicted.

Catherine Mackinnon, aged about fifty, unmarried; Peggy Mackinnon, aged about forty-eight, unmarried; and Catherine Macphee (a half-sister of the two Mackinnons), also unmarried; occupied one house. Catherine Mackinnon was for a long time sick and was confined to bed when the factor and his party came to beat down the house. At first they requested her to get up and walk out but her sisters said was too unwell. They answered, 'Oh, she is scheming.' The sisters said she was not, that she had been ill for a considerable time, and the sick woman herself, said feebly that she was quite unfit to be removed but, that if God spared her and bestowed upon her better health, she would remove of her own accord. This was not good enough; *they forced her out of bed, sick as she was, and left her beside a ditch from 10 a.m. to 5 p.m.,* when, afraid that she would die, they moved her to a house and provided her with cordials and warm clothing. Imagine the sufferings of this poor woman, forced from her sick bed and left exposed beside a cold ditch for seven long hours. Peggy and her half-sister Macphee are still burrowing among the ruins of their old home. There was no hope whatever of Catherine Mackinnon's recovery.

The factor cannot contradict one sentence in this short narrative of the poor females. The melancholy truth of it is too well known in the district to admit of a tenable explanation. Nothing can palliate or excuse such gross inhumanity and it is right and proper that British Christians should be made aware of such cruelty towards helpless fellow-creatures in sickness and distress.

The last case is that of Duncan Robertson, aged thirty-five, his wife, aged thirty-two, and three children. Very poor; the oldest boy is deformed and weak in mind and body, requiring almost constant care from one of his parents. Robertson was warned out like the rest of the tenants and decree of removal was obtained against him. At the levelling time the factor came up with his men before Robertson's door and ordered the inmates out. Robertson pleaded for mercy on account of his sick child. At last the factor sent in one of the officers who, on his return, said that the boy really was an object of pity. The factor said he could not help it, that he must pull down. Some pieces of furniture were then thrown out, and the picks were fixed in the walls, when Robertson's wife ran out and begged them to delay, asking the factor to come in and see her sick child. He replied, 'I am sure I am no doctor.' 'I know that,' she said, 'but God might have given you Christian feelings and compassion.' 'Bring him out here,' said the factor, and the poor mother ran to the bed and brought out her sick boy in her arms. When the factor saw him, he admitted that he was an object of pity but warned Robertson that he must quit Knoydart as soon as possible so that his house would be pulled down about his ears. The levellers peep in once a week to see if the boy is getting better, so that the house may be razed.

We could give additional particulars of the cruelties which had to

119

be endured by the poor wretches who remained, cruelties which would never be tolerated in any other civilized country, but the record would only inflict further pain.

Retribution has overtaken the evictors and is it a wonder that the chiefs of Glengarry are now as little known and own as little of their ancient domains in the Highlands as their devoted clansmen? There is now scarcely one of the name of Macdonald in the wide district once inhabited by thousands. It is a huge wilderness in which barely anything is met but wild animals and sheep and their keepers.

Strathglass

It has been shown that in Glengarry, a chief's widow, during her son's minority, was responsible for the Knoydart evictions in 1853. Another chief's widow, *Marsali Bhinneach* – Marjory, daughter of Sir Ludovick Grant of Dalvey, widow of Duncan Macdonnell of Glengarry, who died in 1788 – gave the whole of Glencruaich as a sheep farm to one south country shepherd. To make room for him, she evicted over five hundred people from their ancient homes. The late Edward Ellice stated before a Committee of the House of Commons in 1873 that, about the time of the rebellion in 1745, the population of Glengarry amounted to between five and six thousand. At that time the glen turned out one soldier in support of Prince Charles for every pound of rental paid to the proprietor. Today it is questionable if the same district could turn out twenty men – certainly not that number of Macdonalds. The bad example of this heartless woman was unfortunately imitated afterwards by her daughter Elizabeth, who, in 1795, married William Chisholm of Chisholm, and to whose evil influence may be traced the great eviction which in 1801 cleared Strathglass almost to a man of its ancient inhabitants. Chisholm was often in bad health and the management of the estate fell into the hands of his hard-hearted wife. Between 1801 and 1803, five thousand, three hundred and ninety people were driven out of these Highland glens; a very portion of them were evicted from Strathglass by the daughter of the notorious *Marsali Bhinneach*. From among the

120

living cargo of one of the vessels which sailed from Fort William, at least fifty-three souls died of an epidemic on the way out. On the arrival of the surviving cargo at Pictou, they were shut in on a narrow point of land, forbidden to communicate with any of their friends who had gone before them, for fear of communicating the contagion. Here they suffered indescribable hardships.

By a peculiar arrangement between the Chisholm who died in 1793 and his wife, a considerable portion of the people were saved for a time from the ruthless conduct of *Marsali Bhinneach*'s daughter and her co-adjusters. Alexander Chisholm married Elizabeth, daughter of a Dr. Wilson, in Edinburgh. He made provision for his wife in case of her outliving him, by which it was left optional with her to take a stated sum annually or the rental of certain townships, or club farms. Her husband died in 1793, when the estate reverted to his half-brother, William. The widow, on the advice of her only child, Mary, chose the joint farms instead of the sum of money named in her marriage settlement and, though great efforts were made by *Marsali Bhinneach's* daughter and her friends, the widow kept the farms in her own hands and took great pleasure in seeing a prosperous tenantry in these townships while all their neighbours were heartlessly driven away. Not one of her tenants was disturbed or interfered with in any way from the death of her husband in February 1793 until her own death in January, 1826, when their farms all came into the hands of the young heir (whose sickly father died in 1817), and his cruel mother. For a few years, the tenants were left in possession but only waiting an opportunity to make a complete clearance of the whole strath. Some had a few years of their leases to run on other parts of the property and could not just then be expelled.

In 1830, every man who held land on the property was requested to meet his chief at the local inn of Cannich. They were all there at the appointed time but no chief came to meet them. The factor soon turned up, however and informed them that the laird had determined to enter into no negotiation or any new arrangements with them that day. They were all in good circumstances, without any arrears of rent, but were practically banished from their homes in the most inconsiderate and cruel manner. It afterwards became known that their farms had been secretly let to sheep farmers from the South.

Mr. Colin Chisholm, who was present at the meeting at Cannich, writes: 'I leave you to imagine the bitter grief and disappointment of men who attended with glowing hopes in the morning but had to tell their families and dependants in the evening that they could see no alternative before them but the emigrant ship, and choosing between the scorching prairies of Australia and the icy regions of North America.' However, the late Lord Lovat, hearing of this, proposed to one of the large sheep farmers on his neighbouring property to give up his farm, offering to give full value for his stock so that he might divide it among those evicted from the Chisholm estate. This arrangement was amicably carried through and at the next Whitsunday – 1831 – the evicted tenants from Strathglass came into possession of the large sheep farm of Glenstrathfarrar and paid over to the late tenant of the farm every farthing of the value set upon the stock by two of the leading valuators in the country. This proved conclusively that the Strathglass tenants were quite capable of holding their own and perfectly able to meet all claims that could be made upon them by their old proprietor. They became very comfortable in their new homes but, about fifteen years after their eviction from Strathglass, they were again removed to make room for deer. On this occasion the late Lord Lovat gave them similar holdings on other portions of his property, and the sons and grandsons of the evicted tenants of Strathglass are now, on the Lovat property, among the most respectable and comfortable middle-class farmers in the county.

The result of the Strathglass evictions was that only two of the ancient native stock remained in possession of an inch of land on the estate of Chisholm. When the present Chisholm came into possession, he found, on his return from Canada, only that small remnant of his own name and clan to receive him. He brought back a few Chisholms from the Lovat property, and re-established on his old farm a tenant who had been evicted nineteen years before from the holding in which his father and grandfather died. The great-grandfather was killed at Culloden, having been shot while carrying his commander, young Chisholm, mortally wounded, from the field. The gratitude of that chief's successors had been shown by his ruthless eviction from the ancient home of his ancestors but it is gratifying to find the present chief making some reparation by bringing back and liberally supporting the representatives of such a devoted follower of his forebears. The present Chisholm, who has the character of being a good landlord, is descended from a distant collateral branch of the family. The evicting Chisholms and their offspring have, every one of them, disappeared, and Mr. Colin Chisholm informs us that there is not a human being now in Strathglass of the descendants of the chief, or of the south country farmers who were the chief instruments in evicting the native population.

Earlier in the history of Strathglass, and towards the end of last century, an attempt was made by south country sheep farmers to persuade Alexander Chisholm to follow the example of Glengarry by clearing out the whole native population. Four southerners, among them Gillespie, who took the farm of Glencruaich, cleared by Glengarry, called upon the Chisholm at Comar and tried hard to convince him of the many advantages which would accrue to him by the eviction of his tenantry and turning the largest and best portions of his estate into great sheep walks, for which they offered to pay him large rents. His daughter, Mary, was then in her teens. She heard the arguments used and, having mildly expressed her objection to the heartless proposal of the greedy southerners, was ordered out of the room, crying bitterly. She found her way to the kitchen, called all the servants together and explained the cause of her trouble. The object of the guests at Comar was soon circulated through the strath and, early the following morning, over a thousand men gathered in front of Comar House and demanded an interview with their chief. This was granted and the whole body of the people remonstrated with him for entertaining, even for a moment, the cruel proceedings suggested by the strangers, whose conduct the frightened natives characterized as infinitely worse than that of the freebooting Lochaber men who, centuries before, had attempted to rob his ancestors of their patrimony but were defeated by the ancestors of those whom it

123

was now proposed to evict out of their native strath. The chief urged calm and suggested that the action they had taken might be seen as an act of inhospitality to his guests, not characteristic of a Highland chief.

The sheep farmers who stood inside the open drawing-room window, heard all that had passed. Seeing the unexpected turn events were taking and the desperate resolve shown by the objects of their cruel purpose, they slipped out by the back door, mounted their horses and galloped away as fast as their steeds could carry them among the hooting and derision of the assembled tenantry. The result of the interview with their laird was a complete understanding between him and his tenants, and the flying horsemen, looking behind them when they reached the top of the Maol Bhuidhe, saw the assembled tenantry forming a procession in front of Comar House and the Chisholm being carried shoulder-high by his stalwart vassals on their way to Invercannich. The pleasant outcome was that chief and clan expressed renewed confidence in each other, a determination to continue in future in the same happy relationship and to maintain all modern and ancient bonds of fealty ever entered into by their respective ancestors.

This turned out to be one of the happiest days that ever dawned on the glen. The people were left unmolested so long as this Chisholm survived – a fact which shows the wisdom of chief and people meeting face to face, and refusing to permit others to cause mischief and misunderstanding between parties whose interests are so closely bound together. This wisdom was ignored after Alexander's death and the result, under the cruel daughter of the notorious *Marsali Bhinneach,* has been already described.

Reference has been made to the Clearance of Glenstrathfarrar by the late Lord Lovat but, for the people removed from there and other portions of the Lovat property, he allotted lands in various other places on his own estates so that, although these changes were difficult for his tenants, His Lordship's proceedings can hardly be called evictions in the ordinary sense of the term. His predecessor, Archibald Fraser of Lovat, however, evicted hundreds from the Lovat estates.

124

Guisachan

The modern clearances which took place within the last quarter of a century in Guisachan, Strathglass, by Sir Dudley Marjoribanks, have been described in all their phases before a Committee of the House of Commons in 1872. The Inspector of Poor for the parish of Kiltarlity wrote a letter which was brought before the Committee, with a statement from another source that 'in 1855, there were 16 farmers on the estate; the number of cows they had was 62 and horses 24; the principal farmer had 2,000 sheep, the next 1,000 and the rest between them 1,200, giving a total of 4,200. Now (1873) there is but one farmer and he leaves at Whitsunday; all these farmers lost the holdings on which they had successfully lived; indeed, it is well known that some of them were able to save some money. They have been sent to the four quarters of the globe, or to vegetate in Sir Dudley's dandy cottages at Tomich, made more for show than convenience, where they have to depend on his employment or charity. To prove that all this is true, take, for instance, the smith and say whether the poverty and starvation were then or now? Under the old *régime,* the smith farmed a piece of land which supplied his family with meal and potatoes; he had two cows, a horse and a score or two of sheep on the hill; he paid £7 in yearly rent; he now has nothing but the bare walls of his cottage and smithy, for which he pays £10. Of course he had his trade then, as he has now. Will he live more comfortably now than he did then?'

It was stated at the same time that, when Sir Dudley Marjoribanks bought the property, there was a population of two hundred and fifty-five souls upon it and, though Sir Dudley threw some doubt upon that statement, he was unable to refute it. When asked, he said that he did not evict any of the people. But when Mr. Macombie said, 'Then the tenants went away of their own free will,' Sir Dudley replied, 'I must not say so quite. I told them that when they had found other places to go to, I wished to have their farms.'

They were, in fact, evicted as much as any others of the ancient tenantry in the Highlands, though it is fair to say that the same harsh cruelty was not applied in their case as in many of the others recorded. Those who had been allowed to remain in the new cottages are without cow, sheep or land, while those alive of those sent off are spread over the world, like those sent from other places.

Glenelg

In 1849, more than five hundred souls left Glenelg. They petitioned the proprietor, Mr. Baillie of Dochfour, to provide means of existence for them at home by means of reclamation and improvements in the district or, failing this, to help them to emigrate. Mr. Baillie eventually chose the latter alternative. A local committee should was appointed to supply him with information as to the number of families willing to emigrate, their circumstances and the amount of aid necessary. He was informed that a sum of £3,000 would be required to land those willing to emigrate at Quebec. This sum included passage money, free rations, a month's sustenance after the arrival of the party in Canada and some clothing for the more destitute. Ultimately, the proprietor offered £2,000 while the Highland Destitution Committee promised £500. There was a great deal of confusion before the *Liscard* finally sailed, regarding the amount of food to be supplied on board, while there were loud protests against sending the people away without any medical man in charge. Thanks to the efforts of the late Mr. Stewart of Ensay, then tenant of Ellanreach on the Glenelg property, who took the side of the people, matters were soon rectified. A doctor was secured and the people satisfied as to the rations to be served during the passage, though these were less than half what was originally promised. On the whole, Mr. Baillie behaved liberally but, considering the suitability of the beautiful valley of Glenelg for arable and food–producing purposes, it is to be regretted that he did not decide to use the labour of the natives to bring the district into a state of cultivation, rather than pay so much to banish them to a foreign land. That they would themselves have preferred this is beyond question.

Mr. Mulock, father of the author of *John Halifax, Gentleman*, an Englishman who could not be charged with any preconceived prejudices or partiality for the Highlanders, travelled at this period through the whole North, and published an account of what he had seen. Regarding the Glenelg business, he says, as to their willingness to emigrate:

'To suppose that numerous families would as a matter of choice sever themselves from their loved soil, abolish all the associations of local and patriotic sentiment, fling to the winds every fond memory connected with the home of vanished generations and blot themselves, as it were, out of the book of home-born happiness, is an hypothesis too unnatural to be encouraged by any sober, well-regulated mind.' To satisfy himself, he called forty to fifty heads of families together at Glenelg who had signed an agreement to emigrate but who did not find room in the *Liscard* and were left behind, reduced to a state of starvation after selling off everything they possessed. 'I asked,' he says, 'these poor, perfidiously treated creatures if, in spite of all their hardships, they were willing emigrants. They all assured me that nothing short of the impossibility of obtaining land or employment at home could drive them to seek the doubtful benefits of a foreign shore. So far from the emigration being, at Glenelg, Lochalsh or South Uist, a spontaneous movement springing out of the wishes of the tenantry, I argue it to be, on the contrary, the product of desperation.' We have no hesitation in saying that this is not only true of those to whom Mr. Mulock specially refers, but to almost all who have left the Highlands for the last sixty years. If a judicious system had been applied of cultivating excellent land, capable of producing food in abundance, in Glenelg, there was not another property in the Highlands on which it was less necessary to send the people away than in that beautiful and fertile valley.

The Hebrides

The people of Skye and Uist, where the Macdonalds for centuries ruled in the manner of princes over a loyal and devoted people, were treated no better than those on the mainland, when their services were no longer required to fight the battles of the Lords of the Isles. *Bha latha eile ann!* There was another day! When possessions were held by the sword, those who wielded them were well cared for. Now that sheepskins are found sufficient, what could be more appropriate, in the opinion of some of the sheepish chiefs of modern times, than to displace the people who anciently secured and held the lands for real chiefs worthy of the name and replace them with the animals that produced the modern sheepskins by which they hold their lands, especially when these were found to be better titles than the old ones – the blood and sinew of their ancient servants.

Prior to 1849, the manufacture of kelp in the Outer Hebrides had been for many years a large source of income to the proprietors of those islands, and a considerable revenue to the inhabitants; the lairds, in consequence, for many years encouraged the people to remain. It is alleged that the population multiplied out of all proportion to the means of subsistence within reach when kelp manufacture failed. To make matters worse for the poor tenants, the rents were meanwhile raised by the proprietors to more than double – not because the land was considered worth more by itself, but because the possession of it enabled the poor tenants to earn a certain sum a year from kelp made out of the sea-ware to which their holdings entitled them and out of which the proprietor pocketed a profit of from £3 to £4 per ton.

North Uist

In 1849 Lord Macdonald determined to evict between six and seven hundred persons from Sollas in North Uist, of which he was then proprietor. They were at the time in a state of great misery from the failure of the potato crop for several years in succession, many of them having had to work ninety-six hours a week for two stones of Indian meal once a fortnight. Sometimes even that miserable dole was not forthcoming and families had to live for weeks solely on shellfish picked up on the shore. Some of the men were employed on drainage works, for which public money was advanced to the proprietors; but here, as in most other places throughout the Highlands, the money earned was used by the factors to wipe off old arrears while the people were left generally to starve. His Lordship decided that they must go and notices of ejectment were served, to take effect on the 15th May, 1849. They asked for delay, to enable them to sell their cattle and other effects to the best advantage at the summer markets, and offered to work meanwhile making kelp on terms profitable to the proprietors if only, in the altered circumstances, they might get their crofts on equitable terms. Their petitions were ignored.

They were directed to sow as much corn and potatoes as they could during that spring. For this, they were to be fully compensated, whatever happened. They sold much of their effects to buy seed and continued to work and sow up to and after the 15th May. They then began to cut their peats as usual, thinking they were after all to be allowed to get the benefit. They were, however, soon disappointed – their goods were mortgaged. Many of them were turned out of their houses, the doors locked, and everything they possessed – cattle, crops, and peats – seized. Even their bits of furniture were thrown out of doors in the manner which had long become the fashion in such cases.

It was too late in the year – towards the end of July – to start for Canada. Before they could arrive there, the cold winter would be upon them and they had neither means nor money to provide against it. They rebelled, and the principal Sheriff-Substitute, Colquhoun, with his officers and a strong body of police, left Inverness for North Uist to eject them from their homes. Unwilling to proceed to extremes, on their arrival at Armadale they sent a messenger ashore to ask for instructions in case of resistance or, if possible, to obtain a modification of His Lordship's views. Lord Macdonald had no instructions to give but referred the Sheriff to Mr. Cooper, his factor, whose answer was that the whole population of Sollas would be evicted if they did not at once agree to emigrate. A few men who obstructed the evictors on a previous occasion were arrested and taken to Lochmaddy. The work of destruction soon commenced. At first no opposition was made by the poor people. An eye-witness, whose sympathies were believed to be with the proprietor, describes some of the proceedings as follows:

'In evicting Macpherson, the first case taken up, no opposition to the law officers was made. In two or three minutes the few articles of furniture he possessed – a bench, a chair, a broken chair, a barrel, a bag of wool and two or three small articles, which comprised his whole household of goods and gear – were turned out to the door, and his bothy left roofless. The wife of the prisoner Macphail (one of those taken to Lochmaddy on the previous day) was the next evicted. Her domestic goods were of the simplest character – the things of greatest value to her being three small children, dressed in nothing more than a single coat of coarse blanketing. They played about her knee, while the poor woman, herself half-clothed, her face bathed in tears, and holding an infant in her arms, assured the Sheriff that she and her children were totally destitute and without food of any kind. The Sheriff at once sent for the Inspector of Poor, and ordered him to place the woman and her family on the poor roll.

'The next house was occupied by very old, infirm people, whom the Sheriff positively refused to evict. He also refused to eject eight other families when he discovered an irregularity in the notices served upon them. The next family ejected led to almost the only instance of real resistance in the history of Highland evictions. This man was a crofter and weaver with a wife and nine children to provide for. At this stage a crowd of men and women gathered on a hill a little distance from the house, raising shouts as the police advanced to help in the work of demolition, accompanied by about a dozen men who had come from the other end of the island to help. The crowd, exasperated at the conduct of their own neighbours, threw stones. The police were then drawn up in two lines. The furniture was thrown outside, the web was cut off the loom and the terrified woman rushed to the door with an infant in her arms, exclaiming in a passionate voice – "Tha m*o chlann air a bhi' air a muirt!*" (My children are to be murdered.). The crowd became excited, stones were thrown at the officers, their assistants were driven from the roof and they had to

130

retire behind the police for shelter. Volleys of stones and other missiles followed. The police charged in two divisions. There were cuts and bruises on both sides. The work of demolition was then allowed to go on without further opposition from the crowd.'

Several heart-rending scenes followed but we shall only give a description of the last which took place on that occasion and which brought about a little delay in the cruel work. In one case it was found necessary to remove the women from the house by force.

'One of them threw herself upon the ground and fell into hysterics, uttering the most doleful sounds and barking and yelling like a dog for about ten minutes. Another, with many tears, sobs and groans put up a petition to the Sheriff that they would leave the roof over part of her house where she had a loom with cloth in it which she was weaving. A third woman, the eldest of the family, attacked an officer with a stick and, missing him, sprang upon him, and knocked off his hat. So violently did this old woman conduct herself that two stout policemen had great difficulty in carrying her outside the door. The excitement was again getting so strong that the factor, seeing the determination of the people and finding that if he continued and took the crops away from those who would not leave even when their houses were pulled down about their ears, they would have to be fed and maintained at the expense of the parish during the forthcoming winter, relaxed and agreed to allow them to occupy their houses until next spring, if the heads of families undertook and signed an agreement to emigrate any time next year, from the 1st February to the end of June. Some agreed to these conditions, but most declined. The people were permitted to go back to their unroofed and ruined homes for a few months longer. Their cattle were, however, mostly taken possession of, and applied to the reduction of old arrears.'

Four of the men were afterwards charged with deforcing the officers, and sentenced at Inverness Court of Justiciary each to four months' imprisonment. The following year the district was completely and mercilessly cleared of all its remaining inhabitants, numbering 603 souls.

The Sollas evictions did not satisfy the evicting craze which His

Lordship afterwards so bitterly regretted. In 1851–53, he, or rather his trustee, determined to evict the people from the villages of Boreraig and Suisinish on the Isle of Skye.

Boreraig and Suisinish, Isle of Skye

Donald Ross, writing as an eye-witness of these evictions, says:

'Some years ago Lord Macdonald incurred debts on his property to the extent of £200,000 sterling and, his lands being entailed, his creditors could not dispose of them, but they placed a trustee over them in order to intercept certain portions of the rent in payment of the debt. Lord Macdonald, of course, continues to have an interest and a surveillance over the property in the matter of removals, the letting of the fishings and shootings and the general improvement of his estates. The trustee and the local factor under him have no particular interest in the property, nor in the people thereon, beyond collecting their quota of the rents for the creditors; consequently the property is mismanaged and the crofter and cottar population is greatly neglected. The tenants of Suisinish and Boreraig were the descendants of a long line of peasantry on the Macdonald estates, and were remarkable for their patience, loyalty and general good conduct.'

The only plea made at the time for evicting them was that of overpopulation. Ten families received the usual summonses, and passages were secured for them in the *Hercules,* an unfortunate ship which sailed with a cargo of passengers under the auspices of a body calling itself 'The Highland and Island Emigration Society'. A deadly fever broke out among the passengers, the ship was detained at Cork, and a large number of the passengers died of the epidemic. After the sad fate of so many of those previously cleared out in the ill-fated ship, it was generally thought that some compassion would be shown for those who had been permitted to remain. Not so, however. On the 4th of April, 1853, they were all warned out of their holdings. They petitioned and pleaded with His Lordship to no purpose. They were ordered to remove their cattle from the pasture and themselves from their houses and lands. They again petitioned His Lordship for his

132

merciful consideration. Eventually they were informed that they would get land on another part of the estate – portions of a barren moor, quite unfit for cultivation.

In the middle of September, Lord Macdonald's ground officer arrived with a body of constables and at once proceeded heartlessly to eject the whole population, numbering thirty-two families. At this time the able-bodied male members of the families were away from home trying to earn something by which to pay their rents, and help to carry their families through the coming winter. In spite of the wailing of the helpless women and children, the cruel work continued as rapidly as possible, and without any apparent compunction. The furniture was thrown out in what had now become the orthodox fashion. The aged and infirm, some of them so frail that they could not move, were pushed or carried out.

'The scene was truly heart-rending. The women and children went about tearing their hair and rending the heavens with their cries. Mothers with babes at the breast looked helplessly on while their effects and their aged and infirm relatives, were cast out and the doors of their houses locked in their faces. The young children, poor, helpless, little creatures, gathered in groups, gave vent to their feelings in loud and bitter wailings. No mercy was shown to age or sex, all were indiscriminately thrust out and left to die on the hills.'

Untold cruelties were perpetrated on this occasion on the helpless creatures during the absence of their husbands and other principal bread-winners.

Donald Ross in his pamphlet, *Real Scottish Grievances*, published in 1854, and who not only was an eye-witness but generously supplied the people with a great quantity of food and clothing, describes several of the cases, including:

Flora Robertson or Matheson, a widow, aged ninety-six, lived with her son, Alexander Matheson, who had a small lot of land in Suisinish. Her son was a widower with four children and, shortly before the time for evicting the people arrived, he went away to labour at harvest in the South, taking his oldest boy with him. The grandmother and the other three children were left in the house.

133

'When the evicting officers and factor arrived, the poor old woman was sitting on a couch outside the house. The day was fine, so her grandchildren lifted her out of her bed and brought her to the door. She was very frail and it would have warmed any heart to see how the two youngest of her grandchildren helped her along. They seated her where there was most shelter, brought her clothing, wrapped her up and tried to make her comfortable. The gratitude of the old woman was unbounded at these little acts of kindness and compassion and the poor children were pleased that their services were appreciated. The sun was shining beautifully, the air was refreshing, the gentle breeze wafted across the hills and, mollified by passing over the waters of Loch Slapin, brought relief and vigour to poor old Flora.

Nothing could exceed the beauty of the scene – the glittering sea, the hills with the heather in full bloom and the wild flowers, the crops of corn beginning to get yellow for the harvest, the small patches of potatoes under flower, the sheep and cattle lying down to rest on the face of the hills, the dogs basking at full length in the sun, the little boats on the loch reflecting their own tiny shadows on the bosom of the deep, still waters. Although Flora's eyes were getting dim with age, she looked on the objects before her with great delight. Her grandchildren brought her warm milk and bread from a neighbour's house and tried to feed her as if she had been a pet bird but the old woman could not take much, although she was invigorated by the change of air. A white fleecy cloud now and then ascended, but the sun soon dispelled it and, with the exception of a stream which passed near the house, making a continuous noise in its progress over rocks and stones, there was nothing above or around to disturb the eye or the ear for one moment. While the old woman was thus enjoying the fresh air and admiring the landscape, and just when the poor children had entered the house to prepare a frugal meal, a sudden barking of dogs warned of the approach of strangers. The natural curiosity of the children was aroused and off they set across the fields and over fences after the dogs. They soon returned, however, with horror on their faces; they had a fearful tale to unfold. The furniture and other effects of their nearest neighbours, just across the

134

hill, they saw thrown out; they heard the children screaming and saw the factor's men putting bars and locks on the doors. The heart of the old woman, so recently revived and invigorated, was about to break. What was she to do? What could she do? Absolutely nothing! The poor children thought that, if they could only get their granny inside before the evicting officers arrived, that would be safe. No one, they thought, would interfere with an old creature of ninety-six and they began to move their grandmother into the house. The officers, however, arrived before they could get this accomplished and they threw every article that was inside the house out of the door and then placed large bars and padlocks on the door! The grandchildren were horror-struck at this procedure. Here they were, shut out of house and home, their father and elder brother several hundred miles away, their mother dead, their grandmother, aged, frail and unable to move, sitting before them, quite unfit to help herself, and with no other shelter than the broad canopy of heaven. Their predicament would have twisted the strongest nerve and tried the stoutest heart, with nothing but helpless infancy and old age and infirmities to meet it. We cannot comprehend the feelings of the poor children on this occasion; and cannot find words strong enough to condemn those who made them homeless. After the grandchildren had cried until they had emptied themselves of tears and exhausted their strength, along with the other children of the district, as house after house was swept of its furniture, the inmates evicted and the doors locked, they returned to their poor old grandmother to console her. But it was getting late and the air was now cold and freezing. The neighbours were all locked out and could give no shelter, and the old woman was unable to travel. The children discussed what to do next: the first consideration was shelter for the first night and, as a sheep-cot was near, the children prepared to move the old woman to it. It was small and damp with no door, no fireplace, no window, no bed but it was better than exposure to the night air. They had overlooked one difficulty, however. The grandmother could not walk and the distance was some hundreds of yards. They could get no help, for all the neighbours were in a similar situation and greatly distressed. In spite of this,

135

the children helped the poor woman sometimes to walk a few yards, sometimes to crawl on her hands and knees, until she at last reached the cot.

The sheep-cot was wretched, quite unfit for human beings, yet here the widow was compelled to remain until December. When her son came home from the harvest in the South, he was amazed at the treatment his aged mother and his children had received. He was then in good health but in a few weeks the cold and damp of the sheep-cot had a deadly effect upon his health. He was seized with violent cramps, then with a cough; at last his limbs and body swelled and he died.

The inspector of poor, who was ground officer to Lord Macdonald and also acted as the chief officer in the evictions, at last appeared and removed the old woman to another house; not, however, until he was threatened with a prosecution for neglect of duty. The grandchildren were also removed from the sheep-cot, for they were ill; Peggy and William were seriously so, but Sandy, although ill, could walk a little. The inspector for the poor gave the children, during their illness, only 14 lbs. of meal and 3 lbs. of rice, as aliment for three weeks, and nothing else. To the grandmother he allowed two shillings and six-pence per month, but made no provision for fuel, lodgings, nutritious diet or medicines, all of which were much needed.

When I visited the house where old Flora Matheson and her grand-children live, I found her lying on a miserable pallet of straw, which, with a few rags of clothing, are on the bare floor. She is reduced to a skeleton and, from her own statement to me in presence of witnesses, coupled with other inquiries and examinations, I have no hesitation in declaring that she was then actually starving. She had no nourishment, no cordials, nothing whatever in the way of food but a few wet potatoes and two or three shellfish. The picture she presented, as she lay on her wretched pallet of rags and straw with her arms completely bare, was a lamentable one, which reflects the deepest discredit on the parochial authorities of the strath. There was no one to help this weak and aged pauper but her grandchild, a young girl of ten years old. Surely in a country boasting of its humanity, liberty and

Christianity, such conduct should no longer be tolerated in dealing with the infirm and helpless poor. The pittance of 2s. 6d. a month is a mockery of the claims of this old woman; it is insulting to the common sense and everyday experience of sensible people, and a shameful evasion of the law. But for acts of charity from other places, Widow Matheson would have died of starvation long before now.

Three men were afterwards charged with deforcing the officers of the law before the Court of Justiciary at Inverness. They were first imprisoned at Portree and afterwards marched over one hundred miles on foot to Inverness. They arrived two days before the date of their trial. The factor and Sheriff officers came in their conveyances, at the public expense, and lived right loyally, confident they would obtain a victory, and get the three men sent to the Penitentiary to wear hoddy, break stones, or pick oakum for at least twelve months. The accused, through the influence of charitable friends, secured the services of Mr. Rennie, solicitor, Inverness, who was able to show to the jury the unfounded and farcical nature of the charges made against them. His eloquent and able address to the jury on their behalf was irresistible, and we cannot better explain the nature of the proceedings than by quoting it in part from the report given of it, at the time, in the *Inverness Advertiser:*

'Before proceeding to comment on the evidence in this case, he would call attention to its general features. It was one of a fearful series of ejectments now being carried through in the Highlands; and it really became a matter of serious reflection, how far the pound of flesh allowed by law was to be permitted to be extracted from the bodies of the Highlanders. Here were thirty-two families, averaging four members each, or from 130 to 150 in all, driven out from their houses and happy homes, and for what? For a tenant who, he believed, was not yet found. But it was the will of Lord Macdonald and of Messrs. Brown and Ballingal that they should be ejected; and the civil law having failed them, the criminal law with all its terrors, is called in to overwhelm these unhappy people. But, thank God, it has come before a jury – before you, who are sworn to return, and will return, an impartial verdict; and which verdict will, I trust, be one

137

that will stamp out with ignominy the cruel actors in it. The Duke of Newcastle had querulously asked, "Could he not do as he liked with his own?" but a greater man had answered, that "property has its duties as well as its rights," and the concurrent opinion of an admiring age testified to this truth.

'Had the factor here done his duty? No! He had driven the miserable inhabitants out to the barren heaths and wet mosses. He had come with the force of the civil power to dispossess them, and make way for sheep and cattle. But had he provided adequate refuge? The evictions in Knoydart, which had lately occupied the attention of the press and all thinking men, were cruel enough; but there a refuge was provided for a portion of the evicted, and ships for their conveyance to a distant land. Would such a state of matters be tolerated in a country where a single spark of Highland spirit existed? No! Their verdict that day would proclaim, over the length and breadth of the land, an indignant denial.

'Approaching the present case more minutely, he would observe that the prosecutor, by deleting from this libel the charge of obstruction, which was passive, had cut away the ground from under his feet. The remaining charge of deforcement being active, pushing, shoving, or striking, was essential. But he would ask, What was the character of the village, and the household of Macinnes? There were mutual remonstrances; but was force used? The only things the officer Macdonald seized were carried out. A spade and creel were talked of as being taken from him, but in this he was unsupported. The charge against the panel, Macinnes, only applied to what took place inside his house. As to the other panels, John Macrae was merely present. He had a right to be there; but he touched neither man nor thing, and he at any rate must be acquitted. Even with regard to Duncan Macrae, the evidence *quoad* him was contemptible. According to Allison, in order to constitute the crime of deforcement, there must be such violence as to intimidate a person of ordinary firmness of character. Now, there was no violence here, they did not even speak aloud, they merely stood in the door; that might be obstruction, it was certainly not deforcement. Had Macdonald, who, it appeared, combined in his single person the triple offices of Sheriff officer, ground officer and inspector of poor, known anything of his business and gone about it in a proper and regular manner, the present case would never have been heard of. As an instance of his irregularity, whilst his execution of deforcement bore that he read his warrants, he stated that he only read part of them. Something was attempted to be made of the fact of Duncan Macrae seizing one of the constables and pulling him away, but this was done in a good-natured manner and the constable admitted he feared no violence. In short, it would be a farce to call this a case of deforcement. As to the general character of the panels, it was irreproachable and their behaviour on that day was their best certificate.'

The jury immediately returned a verdict of 'Not guilty' and the poor Skyemen were dismissed from the bar amid the cheers of an Inverness crowd. The families of these men were evicted the next Christmas in the most spiteful and cruel manner, delicate mothers half-dressed and recently born infants being pushed out into the drifting snow. Their few bits of furniture, blankets and other clothing lay for days under the snow while they found shelter as best they could in broken-down, dilapidated outhouses and barns. These proceedings were afterwards found to have been illegal, the original summonses having been exhausted in the previous evictions when the Macinneses and the Macraes were unsuccessfully charged with deforcing the Sheriff officers. The proceedings were universally condemned by every right-thinking person who knew the district, as most unjustifiable and improper and for 'the reckless cruelty and inhumanity with which they were carried through.' Yet the factor issued a circular in which he coolly informed the public that these evictions were prompted by motives of benevolence, piety and humanity, and that the cause for them all was 'because they (the people) were too far from Church'. Oh God, what crimes have been committed in Thy name, and in that of religion! Preserve us from such piety and humanity as were exhibited by Lord Macdonald and his factor on this and other occasions.

139

A Contrast

Before leaving Skye, it will be interesting to see the difference of opinion which existed among the chiefs regarding the eviction of the people at this period and a century earlier. We have just seen what a Lord Macdonald has done in the present century. Let us compare his proceedings and feelings to those of his ancestor, in 1739, a century earlier. In that year, a certain Norman Macleod managed to get some islanders to emigrate and it was feared that Government would hold Sir Alexander Macdonald of Sleat responsible, as he was reported to have encouraged Macleod.

The baronet was away from home, so his wife, Lady Margaret, wrote to Lord Justice-Clerk Milton on the 1st January, 1740, pleading with him to use all his influence against a prosecution of her husband, which, 'tho' it cannot be dangerouse to him, yett it cannot faill of being both troublesome and expensive.' She begins her letter by stating that she was informed 'by different hands from Edinburgh that there is a currant report of a ship's haveing gone from thiss country with a greate many people designed for America, and that Sir Alexander is thought to have concurred in forceing these people away.' She then declares the charge against her husband to be 'a falsehood', but she is 'quite acquainted with the danger' of a report of that nature. Instead of Sir Alexander being a party to the proceedings of this 'Norman Macleod, with a number of fellows that he had picked up to execute his intentions,' he 'was both angry and concern'd to hear that some of his oune people were taken in thiss affair.'

What a contrast between the sentiments here expressed and those which carried out the modern evictions! And yet it is well known that, in other respects, no more humane man ever lived than he who was nominally responsible for the cruelties in Skye and at Sollas. He allowed himself to be imposed upon by others and completely abdicated his high functions as landlord and chief of his people. We have the most conclusive testimony and assurance from one who knew His Lordship intimately, that, to his dying day, he never ceased to regret what

140

had been done in his name and with his tacit approval, in Skye and in North Uist.

South Uist and Barra

Napoleon Bonaparte, at one time, took five hundred prisoners and was unable to provide food for them. He would not let them go, though he saw that they would die of hunger. His idea of mercy was to have them all shot. Donald Macleod refers to this painful act as follows:

'All the Christian nations of Europe were horrified, every breast was full of indignation at the perpetrator of this horrible tragedy and France wept bitterly for the manner in which the tender mercies of their wicked Emperor were exhibited. Ah! but guilty Christians, you Protestant law-making Britain, tremble when you look towards the great day of retribution. Under the protection of your law, Colonel Gordon has consigned 1,500 men, women, and children to a death a hundred-fold more agonizing and horrifying. With the sanction of your law he (Colonel Gordon) and his predecessors, in imitation of His Grace, the Duke of Sutherland, and his predecessors, removed the people from the land created by God, suitable for cultivation and for the use of man and put it under brute animals. He threw the people upon bye-corners, precipices and barren moors, there exacting exorbitant rack-rents, until the people were made penniless so that they could neither leave the place nor better their condition in it. The potato blight blasted their last hopes of retaining life upon the unproductive patches, so they clamoured for food. Their distress was made known through the public press; public meetings were held and some known knaves blamed the whole misery upon the God of providence. The generous public responded: immense sums of money were placed in the hands of Government agents and other individuals to save the people from death by famine on British soil.

'Colonel Gordon and his worthy allies were silent contributors, though terrified. The gallant gentleman the Home Secretary sought to purchase the Island of Barra for a penal colony, but it would not

141

suit. Yet our humane Government sympathized with the Colonel and his coadjutors and consulted the honourable and brave MacNeil, the chief pauper gauger of Scotland, upon the most effective and speediest scheme to relieve the gallant Colonel and colleagues from this clamour and eyesore, as well as to save their pockets from able-bodied paupers. The result was that a liberal grant from the public money, which had been granted a year before for the purpose of improving and cultivating the Highlands, was made to Highland proprietors to assist them to drain the nation of its best blood and to banish the Highlanders across the Atlantic. There they could die by famine among strangers in the frozen regions of Canada, far from British sympathy, and far from the resting-place of their brave ancestors. This was in total disregard of the importance that the Highlanders, more than any other race of people I have known or read of, place on the idea of burial in their own native soil.

'Consider this helpless, unfortunate people; place yourselves for a moment in their hopeless condition at their embarkation, decoyed, in the name of the British Government, by false promises of assistance, to procure homes and comforts in Canada, which were denied to them at home – decoyed to an unwilling and partial consent. And those who resisted or recoiled from this conditional consent, fleeing to the caves and mountains to hide themselves, look at them, chased and caught by policemen, constables and other underlings of Colonel Gordon, handcuffed and huddled together with the rest on an emigrant vessel. Hear the sobbing, as they are taking their last look and bidding a final adieu to their romantic mountains and valleys, the fertile straths, dales and glens, which their forefathers from time immemorial inhabited, and which were as dear and as sacred to them as their very existence. Follow them on their six weeks' dreary passage, rolling upon the mountainous billows of the Atlantic, ill-fed, ill-clad, among sickness, disease and excrement. Then come ashore with them where death is in store for them; hear the captain giving orders to discharge the cargo of livestock; see the confusion, hear the noise. Hear mothers and children asking fathers and husbands, "Where are we going?" Hear the reply, "*Chan eil fios againn.*" (We know not.) See them, in groups, in search of the Government Agent, who, they were told, was to give them money. Look at their despairing countenances when they come to learn that no agent in Canada is authorized to give them a penny. Hear them praying the captain to bring them back to die among their native hills, so that their ashes might mingle with those of their forefathers. Hear this request refused, and the poor, helpless wanderers bidding adieu to the captain and crew, who showed them all the kindness they could, and to the vessel to which they formed something like an attachment during the voyage. Look at them, scantily clothed, destitute of food, without farming implements, consigned to their fate, carrying their children on their backs, begging as they crawl along in a strange land, unqualified to beg or buy their food for want of English, until the slow-moving, mournful company reach Toronto and Hamilton, in Upper Canada, where, according to all accounts, they spread themselves over their respective burying-places, where famine and frostbitten deaths were awaiting them.

'This is a painful picture, the English language fails to supply me with words to describe it. How can Colonel Gordon, the Duke of Sutherland, James Loch, Lord Macdonald and others of the unhallowed league and abettors, after looking at this sight, remain in Christian communion, ruling elders in Christian Churches, and partake of the emblems of Christ's body broken and shed blood? Can we as a nation be guiltless and allow so many of our fellow-creatures to be treated in such a manner, and not exert ourselves to put a stop to it and punish the perpetrators? Is ambition, which attempted to dethrone God, become omnipotent, or so powerful, when incarnated in the shape of Highland dukes, lords, esquires, colonels and knights that we must submit to its revolting deeds? Are parchment rights of property so sacred that thousands of human beings must be sacrificed year after year till there is no end of such, to preserve them inviolate? Are sheep walks, deer forests, hunting parks and game preserves, so beneficial to the nation that the Highlands must be converted into a hunting desert, and the aborigines banished and murdered? I know that thousands will answer in the negative; yet they will fold their

143

arms in criminal apathy until the extirpation and destruction of my race shall be completed. Fearful is the catalogue of those who have already become the victims of the cursed clearing system in the Highlands, by famine, fire, drowning, banishment, vice and crime.'

He then publishes the following communication from an eye-witness on the enormities perpetrated on South Uist and Barra in the summer of 1851:

'The unfeeling and deceitful conduct of those acting for Colonel Gordon cannot be too strongly censured. The duplicity and art which was used by them in order to entrap the unwary natives is worthy of the craft and cunning of an old slave trader. Many of the poor people were told in my hearing that Sir John McNeil would be in Canada before them, where he would have every necessary prepared for them. Some of the officials signed a document binding themselves to emigrate, in order to induce the poor people to give their names but, in spite of all these stratagems, many of the people saw through them and refused, out and out, to go. When the transports anchored in Loch Boisdale, these tyrants threw off their masks and the work of devastation and cruelty commenced. The poor people were commanded to attend a public meeting at Loch Boisdale, where the transports lay and, according to the intimation, anyone absenting himself from the meeting was to be fined in the sum of £2 sterling. At this meeting some of the natives were seized and, in spite of their entreaties, sent on board the transports. One stout Highlander named Angus Johnston resisted with such pith that they had to handcuff him before he could be mastered but, after the priest's interference, his manacles were removed and he was marched between four officers on board the emigrant vessel. One morning, during the transporting season, we were suddenly awakened by the screams of a young female who had been re-captured in an adjoining house, having escaped after her first capture. We all rushed to the door, and saw the broken-hearted creature, with dishevelled hair and swollen face, dragged away by two constables and a ground officer. Were you to see the racing and chasing of policemen, constables and ground officers pursuing the outlawed natives, you would think that you had been transported to the banks of the Gambia, on the slave coast of Africa.

'The conduct of the Rev. E. Beatson on that occasion is deserving of the censure of every feeling heart. This wolf in sheep's clothing made himself very officious, as he always does when he has an opportunity of oppressing the poor Barra men and of gaining the favour of Colonel Gordon. In fact, he is the most vigilant and assiduous officer Colonel Gordon has. He may be seen in Castle Bay, the principal anchorage in Barra, whenever a sail is hoisted, directing his men, like a gamekeeper with his hounds, in case any of the doomed Barra men should escape. He offered one day to board an Arran boat that had a poor man concealed but the master, John Crawford, lifted a hand-spike and threatened to split the skull of the first man who would attempt to board, and so the poor Barra man escaped their clutches.

'I may state in conclusion that two girls, daughters of John Macdougall, brother of Barr Macdougall, whose name is mentioned in Sir John McNeil's report, have fled to the mountains to elude the grasp of the expatriators, where they still are, if alive. Their father, a frail, old man, along with the rest of the family, has been sent to Canada. The ages of these girls are twelve and fourteen. Others have fled in the same way but I cannot give their names just now.'

We shall now take the reader after these people to Canada, and witness their deplorable and helpless condition and privations in a strange land. The following is extracted from a Quebec newspaper:

'We noticed in our last the deplorable condition of the six hundred paupers who were sent to this country from the Kilrush Unions. We have today a still more dismal picture to draw. Many of our readers may not be aware of the existence of Colonel Gordon, proprietor of large estates on South Uist and Barra, in the Highlands of Scotland. We are sorry to have to introduce him to their notice under circumstances which will not give them a very favourable opinion of his character and heart.

'It appears that his tenants on the above-mentioned estates were on the verge of starvation and had probably become an eyesore to

145

the gallant Colonel. He decided on shipping them to America. What they were to do there was a question he never put to his conscience. Once landed in Canada, he had no further concern about them. Up to last week, some 1,100 souls from his estates had landed at Quebec and begged their way to Upper Canada; it was in the summer season and, having only a daily morsel of food to procure, they probably escaped the extreme misery which seems to be the lot of those who followed them.

'On their arrival here, they voluntarily made and signed the following statement:"We, the undersigned passengers per *Admiral,* from Stornoway, in the Highlands of Scotland, do solemnly depose to the following facts:That Colonel Gordon is proprietor of estates on South Uist and Barra; that among many hundreds of tenants and cottars whom he has sent this season from his estates to Canada, he gave directions to his factor, Mr. Fleming of Cluny Castle, Aberdeenshire, to ship on board of the above-named vessel a number of nearly four hundred and fifty of said tenants and cottars from the estate in Barra; that, accordingly, a great majority of these people, among whom were the undersigned, proceeded voluntarily to embark on board the *Admiral* at Loch Boisdale on or about the 11th August, 1851, but that several of the people who were intended to be shipped for this port, Quebec, refused to proceed on board and, in fact, absconded from their homes to avoid the embarkation. Whereupon Mr. Fleming gave orders to a policeman, who was accompanied by the ground officer of the estate on Barra and some constables, to pursue the people who had run away among the mountains, which they did, and succeeded in capturing about twenty from the mountains and islands in the neighbourhood but only came with the officers on an attempt being made to handcuff them, and that some who ran away were not brought back, in consequence of which four families at least have been divided, some having come in the ships to Quebec, while the other members of the same families are left in the Highlands.

'"The undersigned further declare that those who voluntarily embarked did so under promises to the effect that Colonel Gordon would defray their passage to Quebec, that the Government Emigration Agent there would send the whole party free to Upper Canada, where, on arrival, the Government agents would give there work and, furthermore, grant them land on certain conditions.

'"The undersigned finally declare that they are now landed in Quebec so destitute that if immediate relief be not afforded them, and continued until they are settled in employment, the whole will be liable to perish with want. (Signed) HECTOR LAMONT, and seventy others."

'This is a beautiful picture! Had the scene been laid in Russia or Turkey, the barbarity of the proceedings would have shocked the nerves of the reader but, when it happens in Britain, emphatically the land of liberty, where every man's house, even the hut of the poorest, is said to be his castle, the expulsion of these unfortunate creatures from their homes, the man-hunt with policemen and bailiffs, the violent separation of families, the parent torn from the child, the mother from her daughter, the infamous trickery practised on those who did embark, the abandonment of the aged, the infirm, women and tender children in a foreign land – forms a tableau which cannot be dwelt on for an instant without horror. Words cannot depict the atrocity of the deed. For cruelty less savage, the slave-dealers of the South have been held up to the execration of the world.

'And if, as men, the sufferings of these our fellow-creatures find sympathy in our hearts, as Canadians their wrongs concern us more dearly. The fifteen hundred souls whom Colonel Gordon has sent to Quebec this season have all been supported for the past week, at least, and conveyed to Upper Canada at the expense of the colony and, on their arrival in Toronto and Hamilton, the greater number have been dependent on the charity of the benevolent for a morsel of bread. Four hundred are in the river at present and will arrive in a day or two, making a total of nearly two thousand of Colonel Gordon's tenants and cottars whom the province will have to support. The winter is at hand, work is becoming scarce in Upper Canada. Where are these people to find food?' (The *Quebec Times*)

We take the following from an Upper Canadian paper, describing the position of the same people after finding their way to Ontario:

147

'We have been distressed for some time to witness in our streets so many unfortunate Highland emigrants, apparently destitute and many of them sick from want and other associated causes. It was pitiful the other day to view a funeral of one of these wretched people. It was, indeed, a sad procession. The coffin was constructed of the poorest material: a few rough boards nailed together was all that could be afforded to convey to its last resting-place the body of the homeless emigrant. Children followed in the mournful train; perhaps they followed a brother's bier, one with whom they had played for many a happy day among their native glens. Theirs were looks of indescribable sorrow. They were in rags; their mourning weeds were the shapeless fragments of what had once been clothes. There was a mother too among the mourners, one who had tended the departed with anxious care in infancy and had doubtless looked forward to a happier future in this land of plenty. The anguish of her countenance told too plainly these hopes were blasted and she was about to bury them in the grave of her child.

'There will be many willing to flatter the generous landlord who had spent so much to assist the emigration of his poor tenants. They will give him the misnomer of a *benefactor*, and for what? Because he has rid his estates of the encumbrance of a pauper population.

'Emigrants of the poorer class who arrive here from the Western Highlands of Scotland are often so situated that their emigration is more cruel than banishment. Their last shilling is spent probably before they reach the upper province; they are reduced to the necessity of begging. But, again, the case of those emigrants of whom we speak is made worse by their ignorance of the English tongue. Of the hundreds of Highlanders in and around Dundas at present, perhaps not half-a-dozen understand anything but Gaelic.

'In looking at these matters, we are convinced that, so far from emigration being a panacea for Highland destitution, it is fraught with disasters of unusual magnitude to the emigrant whose previous habits, under the most favourable circumstances, make him unable to take advantage of the industry of Canada, even when brought here free of expense. We may assist these poor creatures for a time, but

148

charity will scarcely stem the hunger of so many for very long. Winter is approaching, and then − but we leave this painful subject for the present.' (*Dundas Warder*, 2nd October, 1851)

The Island of Rum

The island of Rum at one time had a large population, all of whom were weeded out in the usual way. The Rev. Donald Maclean, Minister of the Parish of Small Isles, informs us in *The New Statistical Account* that 'in 1826 all the inhabitants of the Island of Rum, amounting at least to 400 souls, found it necessary to leave their native land, and to seek for new abodes in the distant wilds of our colonies in America. Of all the old residents, only one family remained upon the Island. The old and the young, the feeble and the strong, were all united in this general emigration − the former to find tombs in a foreign land, the latter to encounter toils, privations and dangers, to become familiar with customs and to acquire that to which they had been entire strangers. A similar emigration took place in 1828 from the Island of Muck, so that the parish has now become much depopulated.'

In 1831, the population of the whole parish was 1,015, while before that date it was much larger. In 1851, it was nine hundred and sixteen. In 1881, it was reduced to five hundred and fifty. The total population of Rum in 1881 was eighty-nine souls.

Hugh Miller, who visited the island, describes it and the evictions thus:

'The evening was clear, calm, golden-tinted; even wild heaths and rude rocks had assumed a flush of transient beauty; and the emerald-green patches on the hillsides, barred by the plough lengthwise, diagonally, and transverse, had borrowed an aspect of soft and velvety richness from the mellowed light and the broadening shadows. All was solitary. We could see among the deserted fields the grass-grown foundations of cottages razed to the ground but the valley, more desolate than that which we had left, had not even a single inhabited dwelling; it seemed as if man had left it for ever. The island, eighteen

149

years before, had been divested of its inhabitants, amounting at the time to more than four hundred souls, to make way for one sheep farmer and eight thousand sheep. All the natives of Rum crossed the Atlantic and, at the close of 1828, the entire population consisted of only the sheep farmer and a few shepherds, his servants: the island of Rum had hardly a single family at this period for every five square miles of area which it contained. But depopulation on so extreme a scale was found inconvenient; the place had been rendered too thoroughly a desert for the comfort of the occupant and, on the occasion of a clearing which took place shortly after on Skye, he accommodated some ten or twelve of the ejected families with sites for cottages and pasturage for a few cows on the bit of morass beside Loch Scresort, on which I had seen their humble dwellings. But the whole of the once-peopled interior remains a wilderness, without inhabitants, all the more lonely for the fact that the deserted valleys, with their plough-furrowed patches and ruined heaps of stone, open onto shores as deserted as themselves, and that the wide untrodden sea stretches drearily around.

'The armies of the insect world were sporting in the light this evening by the million; a brown stream that runs through the valley yielded an incessant poppling sound, from the myriads of fish that were ceaselessly leaping in the pools, beguiled by the quick glancing wings of green and gold that fluttered over them. Along a distant hillside there ran what seemed the ruins of a grey-stone fence, erected, says tradition, in a remote age to facilitate the hunting of the deer. There were fields on which the heath and moss of the surrounding moorlands were fast encroaching, that had borne many a successive harvest, and prostrate cottages, that had been the scenes of christenings, and bridals, and blithe New-Year's Days. It all seemed to speak of a place very suitable for man's habitation, in which not only the necessaries but also a few of the luxuries of life might be procured. But nowhere in sight could man or man's dwelling be seen. The landscape was one without figures.

'I do not much like extermination carried out so thoroughly and systematically – it seems bad policy – and I have not changed my opinion of it, in spite of assurances by the economists that there are more than enough people in Scotland still. There are, I believe, more than enough in our workhouses, more than enough on our pauper rolls, more than enough muddled up, disreputable, useless and unhappy in their miasmatic valleys and typhoid courts of our large towns but I have yet to learn how arguments for local depopulation are to be drawn from facts such as these. A brave and hardy people, favourably placed for the development of all that is excellent in human nature, form the glory and strength of a country – a people sunk into an abyss of degradation and misery and in which it is the whole tendency of external circumstances to sink them yet deeper, constitute its weakness and its shame, and I cannot quite see on what principle the ominous increase which is taking place among us in the worse class is to form our solace or apology for the wholesale expatriation of the better.

'It did not seem as if the depopulation of Rum had tended much to anyone's advantage. The single sheep farmer who had occupied the holdings of so many had been unfortunate in his speculations and had left the island; the proprietor, his landlord, seemed to have been as little fortunate as the tenant, for the island itself was on the market. It was rumoured at the time that it was on the eve of being purchased by some wealthy Englishman, who purposed converting it into a deer forest.

'How strange a cycle! Uninhabited originally, save by wild animals, it became at an early period a home of men, who, as the grey wall on the hillside testified, derived, in part at least, their sustenance from the chase. They broke in from the waste the furrowed patches on the slopes of the valleys, they reared herds of cattle and flocks of sheep, their number increased to nearly five hundred souls. They enjoyed reasonable happiness in an imperfect world. They contributed their portion of hardy and vigorous manhood to the armies of the country, and a few of their more adventurous spirits, impatient of the narrow bounds which confined them and a course of life little varied by incident, emigrated to America. Then came the change of system so general in the Highlands and the island lost all its original inhab-

151

itants on a wool and mutton speculation; inhabitants, the descendants of men who had chased the deer on its hills five hundred years before and who, though they recognized some wild island lord as their superior and did him service, had regarded the place as indisputably their own. And now yet another change was on the eve of ensuing and the island was to return to its original state, as a home of wild animals, where a few hunters from the mainland might enjoy the chase for a month or two every year, but which could form no permanent place of human abode. Once more, a strange and surely most melancholy cycle!'

In another place, the same writer asks, 'Where was the one tenant of the island, for whose sake so many others had been removed?' And he answers, 'We found his house occupied by a humble shepherd, who was in charge of the wreck of his property – property no longer his, but held for the benefit of his creditors. The great sheep farmer had gone down under circumstances of very general bearing, which improving landlords had failed to foresee.'

Harris and the other Western Islands suffered in a similar manner. Mull, Tiree and others in Argyllshire are noticed in dealing with that county.

CHAPTER IV

ARGYLLSHIRE

The Argyllshire Clearances

In many parts of Argyllshire, the people have been weeded out just as effectively, even although the process generally was of a milder nature than that adopted in some of the places already described. By some means or other, however, the ancient tenantry have largely disappeared to make room for the sheep farmer and the sportsman. Mr. Somerville, Lochgilphead, writing on this subject, says, 'The watchword of all is exterminate, exterminate the native race. Through this monomania of landlords, the cottar population is all but extinct and the more affluent farmers are undergoing the same process of dissolution.' He then proceeds:

'About nine miles of country on the west side of Loch Awe, in Argyllshire, that formerly maintained 45 families, are now rented by one person as a sheep farm; and in the island of Luing, same county, which formerly contained about 50 substantial farmers, besides cottars, this number is now reduced to about six. The work of eviction began by giving, in many cases, to the ejected population financial and material aid for emigration; but now the people are turned adrift, penniless and shelterless, to seek a precarious subsistence on the seashore, in the nearest hamlet or village, and in the cities, many of whom sink down helpless paupers on our poor roll. Others, festering in our villages, form a formidable vagrant population, who drink our money contributed as parochial relief. This wholesale depopulation is perpetrated, too, in a spirit of invidiousness, harshness, cruelty and injustice, and must eventuate in permanent injury to the moral, political and social interests of the kingdom.

'The immediate effects of this new system are the dissociation of the people from the land; they are virtually denied the right to labour on God's creation. Garden ground and small allotments of land are in great demand by families, and especially by the aged, who can no longer work, for the purpose of keeping cows. By this they might be able to earn an honest, independent maintenance for their families and their children might be brought up to labour instead of growing up vagabonds and thieves. But such, even in our centres of population, cannot be got; the whole is let in large farms and turned into grazing. The few patches of bare pasture, formed by the delta of rivers, the detritus of rocks and tidal deposits are let for grazing at the exorbitant rent of £3 10s. each for a small Highland cow; and the small space to be had for garden ground is equally extravagant. The consequence of these exorbitant rents and the want of agricultural facilities is a depressed, degraded and pauperized population.'

These remarks are only too true, and applicable not only in Argyllshire, but throughout the Highlands generally.

A deputation from the Glasgow Highland Relief Board, consisting of Dr. Robert Macgregor and Mr. Charles R. Baird, their Secretary, visited Mull, Ulva, Iona, Tiree, Coll and part of Morvern in 1849 and they immediately afterwards issued a printed report on the state of these places, from which a few extracts will prove instructive.

The Island of Mull

The population of the Island of Mull, according to the Government Census of 1821, was 10,612; in the Census of 1881, now before us, it is stated at 5,624, or a just over half the of the 1821 figure.

'Tobermory,' we are told, 'has been for some time the resort of the greater part of the small crofters and cottars, *ejected* from their holdings and houses on the surrounding estates, and thus there has been a great accumulation of distress.' Then we are told that 'severe as the destitution has been in the rural districts, we think it has been still more so in Tobermory and other villages' – a telling reply to those who would have us believe that the evictors of those days and of our own were acting as wise benefactors when they ejected the people from the inland and rural districts of the various counties to wretched villages and rocky hamlets on the seashore.

Ulva

The population of the Island of Ulva in 1849 was three hundred and sixty souls. The reporters state that a 'large portion' of it 'has lately been converted into a sheep farm, and consequently a number of small crofters and cottars have been warned away' by Mr. Clark. 'Some of these will find great difficulty in settling themselves any-where, and all of them have little prospect of employment...What-ever may be the ultimate effect to the landowners of the conver-sion of a number of small crofts into large farms, we need scarcely say that this process is causing much poverty and misery among the crofters.' How Mr. Clark carried out his intention of evicting the tenantry of Ulva may be seen from the fact that the population of the island was reduced to fifty-one in 1881.

Kilfinichen

In this district we are told that 'The crofters and cottars having been warned off, 26 individuals emigrated to America at their own expense and one at that of the Parochial Board; a good many removed to Kinloch, where they are now in great pov-erty. Those who remained were not allowed to cultivate any ground for crop or even garden stuffs. The stock and other effects of a number of crofters on Kinloch last year (1848), whose rents averaged from £5 to £15 per annum, were se-questrated and sold, and these parties are now reduced to a state of pauperism, having no employment or means of sub-sistence.' As to the cottars, it is said that 'the great mass of them are now in a very deplorable state.'

155

Gribun

The proprietor of this estate, Colonel Macdonald of Inchkenneth, gave the people plenty of work, by which they were quite independent of relief from any quarter, and the character which he gives to the deputation of the people generally is most refreshing. The reporters state that 'Colonel Macdonald spoke in high terms of the honesty of the people and of their great patience and forbearance under their severe privations.' It is gratifying to be able to record this simple act of justice, not only as the people's due, but specially to the credit of Colonel Macdonald's memory and goodness of heart.

Bunessan

Respecting this district, belonging to the Duke of Argyll, our authority says, 'It will be recollected that the (Relief) Committee, some time ago, advanced £128 to help procure provisions for a number of emigrants from the Duke of Argyll's estate, in the Ross of Mull and Iona, in all 243 persons – 125 adults and 118 children. When there, we made inquiry into the matter and were informed (by those, as it proved, quite ignorant of the facts) that the emigration had been productive of much good, as the parties who emigrated could not find the means of subsistence in this country, and had every *prospect* of doing so in Canada, where all of them had relations, and also because the land occupied by some of these emigrants had been given to increase the crofts of others. Since our return home, however, we have received the distressing news that many of these emigrants had been seized with cholera on their arrival in Canada and that the survivors had suffered great privations.'

Compare the 'prospect' of much good, predicted for these poor creatures, with the sad reality of having been forced away to die a terrible death immediately on arrival on a foreign shore!

156

Iona

Iona, at this time, contained a population of five hundred, reduced in 1881 to two hundred and forty-three. It is the property of the Duke of Argyll.

The Island of Tiree

Tiree is also owned by the Duke of Argyll. The population is given as follows: in 1755 it was 1,509, increasing in 1777 to 1,681; in 1801 to 2,416; in 1821 to 4,181; and in 1841 to 4,687. In 1849, 'after considerable emigrations', it was 3,903, while in 1881 it was reduced to 2,733. The deputation recommended emigration from Tiree as imperative, but they 'call especial attention to the necessity of emigration being conducted on proper principles or on a system calculated to promote the permanent benefit of those who emigrate, and of those who remain, because we have reason to fear that not a few parties in these districts are anxious to get rid of the small crofters and cottars at all hazard, and without making sufficient provision for their future comfort and settlement elsewhere, and because we have seen the very distressing account of the privations and sufferings of the poor people who emigrated from Tiree and the Ross of Mull to Canada this year (1849) and would spare no pains to prevent a recurrence of such deplorable circumstances. As we were informed that the Duke of Argyll had expended nearly £1,200 on account of the emigrants from Tiree, as the Committee advanced £131 15s. to purchase provisions for them and, as funds were remitted to Montreal to carry them up the country, we sincerely trust that the account we have seen of their sufferings in Canada is exaggerated and that it is not, at all events, to be ascribed to lack of suitable provision being made for them before they left this country. Be this as it may, we trust that no emigration will in future be promoted by proprietors or others, which will not secure, as far as human effort can, *the benefit of those who emigrate,* as well as of those who are left at home... Being aware of the poverty of the

157

great majority of the inhabitants of this island, we were agreeably surprised to find their dwellings remarkably neat and clean, such as would bear comparison with cottages in any part of the kingdom. The inhabitants, too, we believe, are active and enterprising and, if given adequate opportunity, would soon raise themselves to comfort and independence.'

The Island of Coll

Separated from Tiree by a channel only two miles wide, Coll had a population in 1755 of 1,193; by 1841 the population was 1,409. At the time of the visit of the deputation, from whose report we quote, the population of the island was down to 1,235, while in 1881 it had fallen to 643. The deputation report that during the destitution the work done by the Coll people 'approximates, if it does exceed, the supplies given'; they are 'hard-working and industrious. . . We saw considerable tracts of ground which we were assured might be reclaimed and cultivated with profit and are satisfied that fishing is a resource capable of great improvement and at which, therefore, many of the people might be employed to advantage; we are disposed to think that, by a little attention and prudent outlay of capital, the condition of the people here might soon be greatly improved. The great difficulty in the way, however, is lack of capital. Mr. Maclean, the principal proprietor, always acted generously when he had it in his power to do so but, unfortunately, he has no longer the ability and the other two proprietors are also under trust.' Notwithstanding these possibilities, the population is undergoing a constant process of diminution.

Ardnamurchan

'*Uaine gu'm mullach*' (Green to their tops!). So Dr. Norman Macleod described the bens of Ardnamurchan in his inimitable sketch, the *Emigrant Ship*, and so they appear even to this day. Their beautiful slopes show scarcely a vestige of heather, but an abundance of rich, sweet grass of a quality eminently suitable for pasturage.

158

As the steamboat passenger sails northward through the Sound of Mull, he sees straight ahead and, stretching at right angles across his course, a long range of low hills culminating in a finely-shaped mass which seems to rise abruptly from the edge of the sea. The hills are those of Ardnamurchan and the dominating pile is Ben Hiant, green to its top. Around the base of the mountain and for miles in every direction, the land is fair, fertile and well adapted either for arable or grazing purposes. It comprises the farm of Mingary, and, today, is wholly under deer.

Down to the second decade of the nineteenth century, Ardnamurchan supported about twenty-six families, which were distributed over the component townships of Coire-mhuilinn, Skinid, Buarblaig and Tornamona. At one sweep, the whole place was cleared, and the grounds added to the adjacent sheep farm of Mingary. The evictions were carried out in 1828, the process being attended with many acts of heartless cruelty on the part of the laird's representatives. In one case a half-witted woman who flatly refused to flit was locked up in her cottage, the door being barricaded on the outside by masonry. She was visited every morning to see if she had arrived at a tractable frame of mind but for days she held out. It was not until her slender store of food was exhausted that she ceased to argue with the inevitable and capitulated. It is to cases of this character that Dr. John MacLachlan, the Sweet Singer of Rahoy, referred in the lines:

> An dall, an seann duine san oinid
> Toirt am mallachd air do bhuaireas.
> (The blind, the aged and the imbecile calling curses
> on thy greed.)

The proprietor at whose instance these 'removals' were carried out was Sir James Milles Riddell, Bart. Of the dislodged families, a few were given small patches of wasteland, some were given holdings in various townships on the estate – the crofts of which were sub-divided for their accommodation – and some were forced to seek sanctuary beyond the Atlantic.

159

Additional clearances were effected on the Ardnamurchan estate in 1853, when Swordle-chaol, Swordle-mhor and Swordle-chorrach, with an aggregate area of about three thousand acres, were divested of their crofting population and thrown into a single sheep farm. Swordle-chaol was occupied by four tenants, Swordle-mhor by six and Swordle-chorrach by six. Five years before the evictions, all the crofters came under a written obligation to the proprietor to build new houses. The walls were to be of stone and lime, 40 ft. long, $17^1/_2$ ft. wide and $7^1/_2$ ft. high. The houses, two gabled, were to have each two rooms and a kitchen, with wooden ceiling and floors, the kitchen alone to be floored with flags. By the end of 1851, the building was completed. Tradesmen had been employed in every case and the cost averaged from £4 to £50. When the people were ejected two years later, they received no compensation for their labours and outlays. They were not even permitted to remove a door, a window or a fixed cupboard. Some of the houses are still intact now, in 1914 and they compare favourably as regards size, design and workmanship with the best and most modern crofter houses in the Ardnamurchan district. The Swordle tenants were among the best-to-do on the estate and not one of them owed the proprietor a shilling in the way of arrears of rent. When cast adrift, the majority of them were assigned 'holdings' of one acre or so in the rough lands of Sanna and Portuairk, where they had to reclaim peatbogs and build houses and steadings for themselves. Sir James Milles Riddell was the proprietor who cleared the Swordles of people in favour of sheep, as well as the Ben Hiant townships, Laga and Tarbert.

About sixteen years ago, Ben Hiant, or Mingary, as well as the Swordles, Laga, Tarbert and other farms, was cleared of sheep and converted into a deer forest covering a total area of 22,000 acres. The native people viewed this change with mild amusement: sheep had been the means of ruining their forefathers, whereas deer had never done them or their kinsfolk the smallest injury.

The highest hill on the estate of Ardnamurchan is Ben Hiant, at an altitude of 1,729 feet. It forms no part of any mountain range, although, when viewed from the sea, it seems to blend with Ben an

Leathaid and other local eminences. For the most part, the elevation of the area embraced in the Ardnamurchan deer forest varies from 600 feet or 700 feet to sea level.

Morven

The population of this extensive parish in 1755 was 1,223, increasing to 2,137 in 1831, but in the Census Returns for 1881 it is stated as 714, or less than one-third of what it was fifty years before.

The late Dr. Norman Macleod, after describing the happy state of things which existed in this parish before the Clearances, says:

'But all this was changed when those tacksmen were swept away to make room for the large sheep farms and when the remnants of the people flocked from their empty glens to occupy houses in wretched villages near the seashore, to become fishers, often where no fish could be caught. The result has been that the Parish, for example, which once had a population of 2,200 souls, and received only £11 per annum from public (Church) funds for the support of the poor, expends now (1863), under the poor law, upwards of £600 annually, with a population diminished by one-half (since diminished to one-third) and with poverty increased in a greater ratio . . . Below these gentlemen tacksmen were those who paid a much lower rent, and who lived very comfortably and shared hospitality with others, the gifts which God gave them. I remember a group of men, tenants in a large glen, which now has not a smoke in it, as the Highlanders say, throughout its length of twenty miles. They had the custom of entertaining in rotation every traveller who cast himself on their hospitality. The host on the occasion was bound to summon his neighbours to the homely feast. It was my good fortune to be a guest when they received the present minister of the Parish while *en route* to visit some of his flock. We had a most sumptuous feast – oatcakes, crisp and fresh from the fire; cream, rich and thick, and more beautiful than nectar; blue Highland cheese, finer than Stilton; fat hens, slowly cooked on the fire in a pot of potatoes, without their skins and with fresh butter – 'stored hens', as the superb dish was

161

called and, though last, not least, tender kid, roasted as nicely as Charles Lamb's cracklin' pig. All was served up with the utmost propriety on a table covered with a fine white cloth and with all the requisites for a comfortable dinner, including the champagne of elastic, buoyant, and exciting mountain air. The manners and conversations of those men would have pleased the best-bred gentleman. Everything was so simple, modest, unassuming, unaffected, yet so frank and cordial. The conversation was such as might be heard at the table of any intelligent man. Alas, there is not a vestige remaining of their homes. I know not whither they are gone, but they have left no representatives behind. The land in the glen is divided between sheep, shepherds and the shadows of the clouds.'

Reminiscences Of A Highland Parish

The Rev. Donald Macleod, editor of *Good Words*, describing the death of the late Dr. John Macleod, the 'present minister of the Parish' referred to by Dr. Norman above and for fifty years minister of Morven, says of the noble patriarch:

'His later years were spent in pathetic loneliness. He had seen his parish almost emptied of its people. Glen after glen had been turned into sheep walks, and the cottages in which generations of gallant Highlanders had lived and died were unroofed, their torn walls and gables left standing like mourners beside the grave and the little plots of garden or of cultivated enclosure allowed to merge into the moorland pasture. He had seen every property in the parish change hands and though, on the whole, kindly and pleasant proprietors came in place of the old families, yet they were strangers to the people, neither understanding their language nor their ways. The consequence was that they perhaps scarcely realized the havoc produced by the changes they inaugurated. "At one stroke of the pen," he said to me, with a look of sadness and indignation, "two hundred of the people were ordered off. There was not one of these whom I did not know, and their fathers before them; and finer men and women never left the Highlands." He thus found himself the sole remaining link between the past and present, the one man above the rank of a peasant who remembered the old days and the traditions of the people. The sense of change was intensely saddened as he went through his parish and passed ruined houses here, there, and everywhere. "There is not a smoke there now," he used to say, with pathos, of the glens which he had known tenanted by a manly and loyal peasantry, among whom lived song and story and the elevating influences of brave traditions. All are gone, and the place that once knew them knows them no more! The hillside, which had once borne a happy people and echoed the voices of joyous children is now a silent sheep walk. The supposed necessities of Political Economy have effected the exchange, but the day may come when the country may feel the loss of the loyal and brave race which has been driven away, and find a new meaning perhaps in the old question, "Is not a man better than a sheep?" They who "would have shed their blood like water" for Queen and country are in other lands, Highland still, but expatriated for ever.

> From the dim shieling on the misty island,
> Mountains divide us and a world of seas,
> But still our hearts are true, our hearts are Highland,
> And in our dreams we behold the Hebrides.
> Tall are these mountains, and these woods are grand,
> But we are exiled from our father's land.
> *Farewell to Fiunary*, by Donald Macleod, 1882.

Glenorchy

Glenorchy, of which the Marquis of Breadalbane is sole proprietor, was ruthlessly cleared of its whole native population. The writer of the *New Statistical Account of the Parish* in 1843, the Rev. Duncan Maclean, '*Fior Ghael*' of the *Teachdaire*, informs us that the census taken by Dr. Webster in 1755, and by Dr. MacIntyre forty years later in 1795, 'differ exceedingly little', only to the number of sixty. The Marquis of the day and his reverence were good friends and one of the apparent results is that the reverend author abstained from giving, in his Account of the Parish the population statistics of the Glenorchy district. It was, however, impossible to pass over that important portion of his duty altogether and, apparently with reluctance, he makes the following sad admission: 'A great and rapid decrease has, however, taken place since (referring to the population in 1795). This decrease is mainly attributable to the introduction of sheep and the absorption of small into large tenements. The native population of the parish of Glenorchy (not of Inishail) has been nearly supplanted by adventurers from the neighbouring district of Breadalbane, who now occupy the far largest share of the parish. There are a few, and only a few, shoots from the stems that supplied the ancient population. Some clans, who were rather numerous and powerful, have disappeared altogether; others, have nearly ceased to exist. The Macgregors, at one time lords of the soil, have totally disappeared; not one of the name is to be found among the population. The Macintyres, at one time extremely numerous, are likewise greatly reduced.'

By this nobleman's mania for evictions, the population of Glenorchy was reduced from 1,806 in 1831 to 831 in 1841. It is, however, gratifying to find that it has since, under wiser management, very largely increased.

In spite of all this we have been seriously told that there has been no DEPOPULATION OF THE COUNTY in the rural districts. In this connection some very extraordinary public utterances were recently made by two gentlemen closely connected with the county of Argyll, attempting to explain away statements made in the House of Commons by Mr. D. H. Macfarlane, M.P., to the effect that the rural population was, from various causes, fast disappearing from the Highlands. One of these utterances was by the Duke of Argyll, who published his remarkable propositions in *The Times*; the other by Mr. John Ramsay, M.P., the Islay distiller, who imposed his baseless statement on his brother members in the House of Commons. These oracles should have known better. They have clearly taken no trouble whatever to ascertain the facts for themselves or have kept them back so that the public might be misled on a question with which the personal interests of both are largely mixed up.

In 1831, the population of the county of Argyll was 100,973 but by 1881 it was down to 76,468. Of the latter number, the Registrar General classifies 30,387 as urban, or the population of 'towns and villages', leaving us only 46,081 as the total rural population of the county of Argyll at the date of the last Census, in 1881. In 1911, the total population for the county had dropped to 70,902.

We must keep in mind that in 1831 the county could not be said to have had many 'town and village' inhabitants; not more than from 12,000 to 15,000. These resided chiefly in Campbeltown, Inveraray and Oban and, if we deduct from the total population for that year, numbering 100,973, even the larger estimate, 15,000, of an urban or town population, we have still left, in 1831, an actual rural population of 85,973. In other words, the rural population of Argyllshire was reduced in fifty years from 85,973 to 46,081.

The increase of the urban or town population is going on at a fairly rapid rate, Campbeltown, Dunoon, Oban, Ballachulish, Blairmore and Strone, Innellan, Lochgilphead, Tarbet and Tighnabruaich combined, having added no less than some 5,500 to the population of the county in the ten years from 1871 to 1881. These populous places will be found respectively in the parishes of Campbeltown, Lismore and Appin, Dunoon and Kilmun, Glassary, Kilcalmonell and Kilbery and in Kilfinan.

In many places the population was larger prior to 1831 than at that date. The state of the population given in 1831 was before the famine of 1836, while that in 1841 comes during a period in which large numbers were sent away to the Colonies. There was no famine between 1851 and 1881, a time during which the population was reduced from 88,567 to 76,468, in spite of the great increase which took place simultaneously in the 'town and village' section of the people in the county.

CHAPTER V

$\mathcal{B}$UTESHIRE

The Arran Clearances

Once upon a time (in 1828), Alexander, tenth Duke of Hamilton, decided to make large farms on his estate and, of course, the will of a duke in his own domain must be respected, even though, as in one instance, the land rented by twenty-seven families was converted into one farm.

The islanders had for many years been discontented and there seemed no hope of a change for the better. If a man worked his place in a progressive way and made improvements on the farm, the benefit accrued solely to the landed proprietor, who thanked the good tenant by raising his rent. If the farmer objected to paying more rent, he would be turned off his holding at the expiration of his lease; then the landlord would collect the increased rent from the new tenant.

So when the duke proposed to a large number of his tenants that, if they would make room for him by leaving their ancestral homes in Arran, he would see that they were well provided for in the New World, it is not surprising that they agreed. It is so nice, when you are cast out, to be told where you can go and directed what to do. The Duke promised to secure for each family a grant of 100 acres of land in Canada, and the same amount of land for each son in each family who at that time had reached the age of twenty-one.

Arriving at their destination at Johnston Ford, province of Quebec, each family constructed a tent by stretching blankets, quilts, etc., over poles, tied together at the top with withes and ropes. Fortunately, the weather was warm and fires were needed only for cooking. In spite of the Duke of Hamilton's promise of 100 acres for each family and each young man who had attained his majority, when the colony was actually on the scene, the Government officials refused to give a grant except to the heads of the families.

The matter of grants has been so variously stated that it is difficult to determine what the conditions were, but it appears that the actual agreement of the Duke of Hamilton was that grants should be given for two years only. Those who came out in 1829 and 1830 secured certain grants after a delay. Those, who did not arrive till 1831 were told by the agents that grants were no longer to be had.

CHAPTER VI

$\mathcal{P}$ERTHSHIRE

Rannoch

Regarding the state of matters in Rannoch a correspondent writes us as follows:

'I am very glad to learn that you are soon to publish a new edition of your *Highland Clearances*. You have done good work already in rousing the conscience of the public against the conduct of certain landlords in the Highlands who, long before now, should have been held up to public scorn and execration, as the best means of deterring others from pursuing a policy which has been so fatal to the best interests of our beloved land.

'. . . In 1851, the population of the district known as the *quod sacra* parish of Rannoch numbered altogether 1,800; at the census of 1881 it was below 900. Even in 1851 it was not nearly what it was earlier. Why this constant decrease? Several no doubt left the district voluntarily but the great bulk of those who left were evicted.

'Take, first, the Slios Min, north side of Loch Rannoch. Fifty years ago the farm of Ardlarich, near the west end, was tenanted by three farmers, who were in good circumstances. These were turned out to make room for one large farmer, who was turned out last year, penniless. The farm is now tenantless. The next place, further east, is the township of Killichoan, containing about thirty to forty houses, with small crofts attached to each.

'The crofters here are very comfortable and happy and their houses and crofts are models of what industry, thrift and good taste can effect. Further east is the farm of Liaran, now tenantless. Fifty years ago it was farmed by seven tenants who were turned out to make room for one man, and that at a lower rent than was paid by the former tenants. Further, in the same direction, there are Aulich, Craganour and Annat, every one of them tenantless. These three farms, lately in the occupation of one tenant, and for which he paid a rental of £900, at one time maintained fifty to sixty families in comfort, all of whom have vanished or were virtually banished from their native land.

'It is only right to say that the present proprietor is not responsible for the eviction of any of the smaller tenants; the deed was done before he came into possession. On the contrary, he is very kind to his crofter tenantry but, unfortunately for him, he inherits the fruits of a bad policy which has been the ruin of the Rannoch estates.

'Then take the Slios Garbh, south side of Loch Rannoch. Beginning in the west end, we have Georgetown, which, about fifty years ago, contained twenty-five or twenty-six houses, every one of which were knocked down by the late laird of Struan, and the people evicted. The crofters of Finnart were ejected in the same way. Next comes the township of Camghouran, a place pretty similar to Killichoan but smaller. The people are very industrious, clean and fairly comfortable, a credit to themselves and the present proprietor. Next comes Dall, where there used to be a number of tenants, now in the hands of an Englishman. The estate of Innerhaden comes next. It used to be divided into ten lots – two held by the laird, and eight by as many tenants. The whole is now in the hands of one family. The rest of Bun-Rannoch includes the estates of Dalchosnie, Lassintullich and Crossmount, where there used to be a large number of small tenants, most of them well-to-do, now held by five.

'Lastly, take the north side of the river Dubhag, which flows out from Loch Rannoch, and is erroneously called the Tummel. Kinloch, Druimchurn and Druimchaisteil, always in the hands of three tenants, are now held by one. Drumaglass contains a number of smallholdings, with good houses on many of them. Balmore, which always had six tenants in it, has now only one, the remaining portion of it being laid out in grass parks. Ballintuim, with a good house upon it, is tenantless. Auchitarsin, where there used to be twenty houses, is

169

now reduced to four. The whole district from, and including, Kinloch to Auchitarsin, belongs to General Sir Alastair Macdonald of Dalchosnie, Commander of Her Majesty's Forces in Scotland. His father, Sir John had taken a great delight in having a numerous, thriving and sturdy tenantry on the estates of Dalchosnie, Kinloch, Lochgarry, Dunalastair and Morlaggan. On one occasion his tenant of Dalchosnie offered to take from Sir John on lease all the land on the north side of the river. "Ay, man," said he, "you would take all that land, would you, and turn out all my people! Who would I get, if my house took fire, to put it out?"

'The present proprietor has virtually turned out the great bulk of those that Sir John had loved so well. Though, it is said, he did not evict any man directly, he is alleged to have made their positions so hot for them that they had to leave. Sir John could have raised hundreds of Volunteers on his estates – men who would have died for the gallant old soldier. But how many could now be raised by his son? Not a dozen men; though he goes about inspecting Volunteers and praising the movement officially throughout the length and breadth of Scotland.'

The author of the *New Statistical Account*, writing of the Parish of Fortingall, of which the district referred to by our correspondent forms a part, says: 'At present (1838) no part of the parish is more populous than it was in 1790; whereas in several districts, the population has since decreased one-half; and the same will be found to have taken place, though not perhaps in so great a proportion, in most or all of the pastoral districts of the county.'

According to the Census of 1801, the population was 3,875 but by 1881 it was reduced to 1,690.

Upwards of 120 families, the same writer says, 'crossed the Atlantic from this parish, since the previous Account was drawn up (in 1791), besides many individuals of both sexes; while many others have sought a livelihood in the Low Country, especially in the great towns of Edinburgh, Glasgow, Dundee, Perth, Crieff and others. The system of uniting several farms together, and letting them to one individual, has more than any other circumstance, produced this result.

Breadalbane

Mr. R. Alister, author of *Barriers to the National Prosperity of Scotland,* had a controversy with the Marquis of Breadalbane in 1853 about the eviction of his tenantry. In a letter dated July of that year, Mr. Alister made a charge against His Lordship, as follows:

'Your lordship states that in reality there has been no depopulation of the district. This, and other parts of Your Lordship's letter, would certainly lead any who know nothing of the facts to suppose that there had been no clearings on the Breadalbane estates; whereas it is generally believed that your lordship removed, since 1834, no less than 500 families! Some may think this is a small matter but I do not. I think it is a great calamity for a family to be thrown out, destitute of the means of life, without a roof over their heads, and cast upon the wide sea of an unfeeling world. In Glenqueich, near Amulree, some sixty families formerly lived, where there are now only four or five, and in America, there is a glen inhabited by its ousted tenants and called Glenqueich still. Yet it is maintained there has been no depopulation here! The desolations here look like the ruins of Irish cabins, although the people of Glenqueich were always characterized as being remarkably thrifty, economical, and wealthy. On the Braes of Taymouth, at the back of Drummond Hill, and at Tullochyoule, some forty or fifty families formerly resided where there is not one now! Glenorchy, by the returns of 1831, showed a population of 1,806; in 1841, 831; is there no depopulation there? Is it true that in Glen Etive there were sixteen tenants a year or two ago, where there is not a single one now? Is it true, My Lord, that you purchased an island on the west coast called Luing, where some twenty-five families lived at the beginning *of this year,* but who are now cleared off to make room for one tenant, for whom an extensive steading is now being erected? If my information is correct, I shall let the public draw their own conclusions. From all that I have heard, I believe that Your Lordship has done more to exterminate the Scottish peasantry than any man now living and perhaps you ought to be ranked next to the Marquis of Stafford in the unenviable clearing celebrities. If I have over-estimated the Clearances at 500 families, please to correct me.' His Lordship thought it prudent not to make the attempt.

In another letter the same writer says:

'You must be aware that your late father raised 2,300 men during the last war, and that 1,600 of that number were from the Breadalbane estates. My statement is that 150 could not *now* be raised. Your Lordship has most carefully evaded all allusion to this, perhaps the worst charge of all. From Your Lordship's silence, I am surely justified in concluding that you may try to evade the question but you dare not attempt an open contradiction. I have often made enquiries of Highlanders on this point and the number above stated was the *highest* estimate. Many who should know state to me that Your Lordship would not get *fifty* followers from the whole estates, and another says, "Why, he would not get half-a-dozen, and not one of them unless they could not possibly do otherwise." This, then, is how matters stand: in 1793–94, there was such a numerous, hardy, and industrious population on the Breadalbane estates, that the number of brave men available to defend their country numbered 1,600; highest estimate now 150; highest banished 1,450. *Per contra* – game of all sorts increased a hundred-fold.'

Those best acquainted with the Breadalbane estates assert that, on the whole property, at least 500 families, or about 2,500 souls, were driven into exile by the hard-hearted Marquis of that day.

It is gratifying to know that the present Lord Breadalbane, who is descended from a different and remote branch of the family, is an excellent landlord, and takes an entirely different view of his duties and relationship to the tenants on his vast property.

CHAPTER VII

NOTABLE DICTA

A Highland Sheriff

Mr. Robert Brown, Sheriff-Substitute of the Western District of Inverness-shire, in 1806 wrote a pamphlet of one hundred and twenty pages entitled 'Strictures and Remarks on the Earl of Selkirk's Observations on the Present State of the Highlands of Scotland'. In this work, a powerful argument against the forced depopulation of the country, he says:

'In the year 1801, a Mr. George Dennon from Pictou carried out two cargoes of emigrants from Fort William to Pictou, consisting of about seven hundred souls. A vessel sailed the same season from Isle Martin with about one hundred passengers, it is believed, for the same place. No more vessels sailed that year but, in 1802, eleven large ships sailed with emigrants to America. Of these, four were from Fort William, one from Knoydart, one from Isle Martin, one from Uist, one from Greenock. Five of these were bound for Canada, four for Pictou and one for Cape Breton. The only remaining vessel, which took a cargo of people in Skye, sailed for Wilmington in the United States. In the year 1803, exclusive of Lord Selkirk's transport, eleven cargoes of emigrants went from the North Highlands. Of these, four were from the Moray Firth, two from Ullapool, three from Stornoway and two from Fort William. The whole of these cargoes were bound for the British settlements and most of them were discharged at Pictou.'

Soon after, several other vessels sailed from the North West Highlands, with emigrants, for the British Colonies. In addition to these,

Lord Selkirk took two hundred and fifty from South Uist in 1802, and in 1803 he sent out to Prince Edward Island about eight hundred souls in three different vessels, most of whom were from the Island of Skye and the remainder from Ross-shire, North Argyll, the interior of the County of Inverness and the Island of Uist. In 1804, 1805 and 1806, several cargoes of Highlanders left Mull, Skye and other Western Islands, for Prince Edward Island and other North American Colonies. Altogether, not less than 10,000 souls left the West Highlands and Isles during the first six years of the present century, a fact which will now appear incredible.

The Wizard of the North

Sir Walter Scott writes: 'In too many instances the Highlands have been drained, not of their superfluity of population, but of the whole mass of the inhabitants, dispossessed by an unrelenting avarice, which will be one day found to have been as short-sighted as it is unjust and selfish. Meantime, the Highlands may become the fairy ground for romance and poetry or the subject of experiment for the professors of speculation, political and economical. But if the hour of need should come – and it may not, perhaps, be far distant – the pibroch may sound through the deserted region, but the summons will remain unanswered.'

A French Economist

The following remarks by the celebrated French economist, M. de Lavaleye, will prove interesting. There is no greater living authority on land tenure than this writer and, being a foreigner, his opinions are not open, as the opinions of our own countrymen may be, to the suspicion of political bias or partisanship on a question which is of universal interest all over the world. Referring to land tenure in this country, he says:

'The dispossession of the old proprietors, transformed by time into new tenants, was effected on a larger scale by the "clearing of estates". When a lord of the manor, for his own profit, wanted to turn

174

the smallholdings into large farms or into pasturage, the small cultivators were of no use. The proprietors adopted a simple means of
getting rid of them and, by destroying their dwellings, forced them
into exile. The classical land of this system is Ireland, or more particularly the Highlands of Scotland.

'It is now clearly established that in Scotland, just as in Ireland, the
soil was once the property of the clan or sept. The chiefs of the clan
had certain rights over the communal domain but they were even
further from being proprietors than was Louis XIV from being proprietor of the territory of France. By successive encroachments, however, they transformed their authority of suzerain into a right of private ownership, without even recognizing in their old co-proprie-
tors a right of hereditary possession. In a similar way the Zemindars
and Talugdars in India were, by the Act of the British Government,
transformed into absolute proprietors. Until modern days, the chiefs
of the clan were interested in retaining a large number of vassals, as
their power, and often their security, were only guaranteed by their
arms. But when the order was established, and the chiefs – or lords, as
they now were – began to reside in the towns, and required large
revenues rather than numerous retainers, they endeavoured to introduce large farms and pasturage.

'We may follow the first phases of this revolution, which com-
mences after the last rising under the Pretender, in the works of
James Anderson and James Stuart. The latter tells us that in his time –
in the last third of the 18th century – the Highlands of Scotland still
presented a miniature picture of the Europe of four hundred years
ago. The rent (so he misnames the tribute paid to the chief of the
clan) of these lands is very little in comparison with their extent, but
if it is regarded relatively to the number of mouths which the farm
supports, it will be seen that land in the Scotch Highlands supports
perhaps twice as many persons as land of the same value in a fertile
province. When, in the last thirty years of the 18th century, they
began to expel the Gaels, they at the same time forbade them to
emigrate to a foreign country, so as to compel them by these means
to congregate in Glasgow and other manufacturing towns.

175

'In his observations on Smith's *Wealth of Nations,* published in 1814, David Buchanan gives us an idea of the progress made by the clearing of estates. "In the Highlands," he says, "the landed proprietor, without regard to the hereditary tenants (he wrongly applies this term to the clansmen who were joint proprietors of the soil), offers the land to the highest bidder, who, if he wishes to improve the cultivation, is anxious for nothing but the introduction of a new system. The soil, dotted with small peasant proprietors, was formerly well populated in proportion to its natural fertility. The new system of improved agriculture and increased rents demands the greatest net profit with the least possible outlay and, with this object, the cultivators are got rid of as being of no further use. Thus cast from their native soil, they go to seek their living in the manufacturing towns."

'George Ensor, in a work published in 1818, says, "They (the landed proprietors of Scotland) dispossessed families as they would grub up coppice-wood, and they treated the villages and their people as Indians harassed with wild beasts do in their vengeance on a jungle with tigers."

'Is it credible, that in the 19th century, in this missionary age, in this Christian era, man shall be bartered for a fleece or a carcase of mutton – nay, held cheaper?. . . Why, how much worse is it than the intention of the Moguls, who, when they had broken into the northern provinces of China, proposed in Council to exterminate the inhabitants, and convert the land into pasture? This proposal, many Highland proprietors have effected in their own country against their own countrymen.

'M. de Sismondi has rendered celebrated on the Continent the famous clearing executed between 1814 and 1820 by the Duchess of Sutherland. More than three thousand families were driven out and 800,000 acres of land, which formerly belonged to the clan, were transformed into seignorial domain. Men were driven out to make room for sheep. The sheep are now replaced by deer and the pastures converted into deer forests, which are treeless solitudes. The *Economist* of 2nd June, 1866, said on this subject: Feudal instincts have as full career now as in the time when the Conqueror destroyed thirty-

176

six villages to make the New Forest. Two millions of acres, comprising most fertile land, have been changed into desert. The natural herbage in Glen Tilt was known as the most succulent in Perth; the deer forest of Ben Alder was the best natural meadow of Badenoch; the forest of Black Mount was the best pasturage in Scotland for black-wooled sheep. The soil thus sacrificed for the pleasures of the chase extends over an area larger than the county of Perth. The land in the new Ben Alder forest supported 15,000 sheep; and this is but the thirtieth part of the territory sacrificed and thus rendered as unproductive as if it were buried in the depths of the sea.

'The destruction of small property is still going on, no longer by encroachment but by purchase. Whenever land comes on to the market, it is bought by some rich capitalist, because the expenses of legal enquiry are too great for a small investment. Thus, large properties are consolidated and fall into mortmain, in consequence of the law of primogeniture and entails. In the 15th century, according to Chancellor Fortescue, England was quoted throughout Europe for its number of proprietors and the comfort of its inhabitants. In 1688, Gregory King estimates that there were 180,000 proprietors, exclusive of 16,560 proprietors of noble rank. In 1786, there were 250,000 proprietors of England. According to the "Domesday Book" of 1876, there were 170,000 rural proprietors in England owning above an acre, 21,000 in Ireland and 8,000 in Scotland. A fifth of the entire country is in the hands of 523 persons. Are you aware, said Mr. Bright in a speech delivered at Birmingham, 27th August, 1866, that one-half of the soil of Scotland belongs to ten or twelve persons? Are you aware of the fact that the monopoly of landed property is continually increasing and becoming more and more exclusive?

'In England, then, as at Rome, large property has swallowed up small property, in consequence of a continuous evolution unchecked from the beginning to the end of the nation's history and the social order seems to be threatened, just as in the Roman Empire.

'An ardent desire for a more equal division of the produce of labour inflames the labouring classes and passes from land to land. In England, it arouses agitation among the industrial classes and is be-

177

ginning to invade the rural districts. It obviously menaces landed property as constituted in this country. The labourers who till the soil will claim their share in it and, if they fail to obtain it here, will cross the sea in search of it. To retain a hold on them, they must be given a vote and there is fresh danger in increasing the number of electors while that of proprietors diminishes, and maintaining laws which renders inequality greater and more striking, while ideas of equality are assuming more formidable sway. To make the possession of the soil a closed monopoly and to augment the political powers of the class who are rigidly excluded is at once to provoke levelling measures and to facilitate them. Accordingly, we find that England is the country where the scheme of the nationalization of the land finds most adherents and is most widely proclaimed. The country which is furthest from the primitive organizations of property is likewise the one where the social order seems most menaced.'

Mr. Joseph Chamberlain

In a speech delivered at Inverness on 18th September, 1885, Mr. Joseph Chamberlain said:

'The history of the Highland Clearances is a black page in the account with private ownership in land and, if it were to form a precedent; if there could be any precedent for wrong-doing; if the sins of the fathers ought to be visited upon the children, we should have an excuse for more drastic legislation than any which the wildest reformer has ever proposed. Thousands of industrious, hard-working, God-fearing people were driven from the lands which had belonged to their ancestors and which, for generations, they had cultivated; their houses were unroofed and destroyed, they were turned out homeless and forlorn, exposed to the inclemency of the winter season, left to perish on the hillsides or to swell the full flood of misery and destitution in the cities to which they were driven for refuge. In some cases, the cruel kindness of their landlords provided the means of emigration, in some cases they were actually driven abroad. They suffered greatly in foreign countries, being unprovided

178

with the means of sustaining themselves until they could earn a livelihood, but the descendants of those who survived have contributed in no mean degree to the prosperity of the countries in which they finally settled. Those who remained behind had, I am afraid, little cause to be grateful for the consideration which was shown to them. In the course of years, they were deprived of all the advantages which they had previously enjoyed. They had never had legal security of tenure. They were transferred from their original holdings in the glens and straths, which at one time resounded with their industry and they were placed upon barren patches on the seashore, where it was impossible for the most exacting toil and industry to obtain a subsistence. The picture that I have drawn was no doubt relieved in some cases by the exceptional generosity and kindness of particular proprietors but, speaking generally, I think it is the fact that the Highland country was to a considerable extent depopulated by those Clearances. The general condition of the people suffered and it has gone on deteriorating until it has become at last a matter of national concern. If I am correct in the statement in which I have endeavoured to summarize what I have read and learned upon this subject, I ask you whether it is not time that we should submit to careful examination and review a system which places such vast powers for evil in the hands of irresponsible individuals and which makes the possession of land not a trust but a means of extortion and exaction?'

Hardships Endured by First Emigrants

The reader is already acquainted with the misery endured by those evicted from Barra and South Uist by Colonel Gordon, after their arrival in Canada. We shall here give a few instances of the unspeakable suffering of those pioneers who left so early as 1773, in the ship *Hector*, for Pictou, Nova Scotia. The *Hector* was owned by two men, Pagan and Witherspoon, who bought three shares of land in Pictou and they engaged a Mr. John Ross as their agent to accompany the vessel to Scotland, to bring out as many colonists as could be induced, by misrepresentation and falsehoods, to leave their homes.

179

They offered free passage, a farm and a year's free provisions to their dupes. On his arrival in Scotland, Ross drew a glowing picture of the land and other manifold advantages of the country.

The Highlanders knew nothing of the difficulties awaiting them in a land covered over with a dense unbroken forest and, tempted by the prospect of owning splendid farms of their own, they were imposed upon by his promise. Many of them agreed to accompany him across the Atlantic and embraced his proposals. At Greenock, three families and five single young men joined the vessel; she then sailed to Lochbroom, in Ross-shire, where she received 33 families and 25 single men, the whole of her passengers numbering about 200 souls. This band, at the beginning of July, 1773, bade a final farewell to their native land, not a soul on board having ever crossed the Atlantic except a single sailor and John Ross, the agent. As they were leaving, a piper came on board who had not paid his passage; the captain ordered him ashore but the strains of the national instrument affected those on board so much that they pleaded to have him allowed to accompany them and offered to share their rations with him in exchange for his music during the passage. Their request was granted and his performances, in no small degree, cheered the noble band of pioneers in their long voyage of eleven weeks in a miserable hulk across the Atlantic.

The pilgrim band kept up their spirits as best they could by song, pipe-music, dancing, wrestling and other amusements. The ship was so rotten that the passengers could pick the wood out of her sides with their fingers. The accommodation was wretched; smallpox and dysentery broke out among the passengers. Eighteen of the children died and were committed to the deep amidst such anguish and heart-rending agony as only a Highlander can understand. Their stock of provisions became almost exhausted, the water became scarce and bad; the remnant of provisions left consisted mainly of salt meat, which, from the scarcity of water, added greatly to their sufferings. The oat-cake carried by them became mouldy, so that much of it had been thrown away before they dreamed of having such a long passage. Fortunately for them, one of the passengers, Hugh Macleod, more

180

prudent than the others, gathered up the despised scraps into a bag and, during the last few days of the voyage, his fellows were glad to join him in devouring this refuse to keep souls and bodies together.

At last the *Hector* dropped anchor in the harbour opposite where the town of Pictou now stands. Though Highland dress was then proscribed at home, this emigrant band carried theirs along with them and, in celebration of their arrival, many of the younger men donned their national dress, to which a few of them were able to add the *sgian dubh* and the claymore. The piper blew his pipes with might and main, its thrilling tones, for the first time, startling the denizens of the endless forest and its echoes resounding through the wild solitude. Scottish emigrants are admitted upon all hands to have given its backbone of moral and religious strength to the Province and to those brought over from the Highlands in this vessel is due the honour of being in the forefront.

But how different was the reality to the expectations of these poor creatures, led by the plausibility of the emigration agent, to expect free estates on their arrival?

The whole scene, as far as the eye could see, was a dense forest. They crowded on the deck to take stock of their future home and their hearts sank within them. They were landed without the provisions promised, without shelter of any kind, and were only able, by the aid of those few before them, to erect camps of the rudest and most primitive description, to shelter their wives and their children from the elements. Their feelings of disappointment were most bitter, when they compared the actual facts with the free farms and the comfort promised them by the lying emigration agent. Many of them sat down in the forest and wept bitterly. Hardly any provisions were possessed by the few who were before them and what there was among them was soon devoured, making all – old and new comers – almost destitute. It was now too late to raise any crops that year. To make matters worse, they were sent some three miles into the forest, so that they could not even take advantage with the same ease of any fish that might be caught in the harbour. The whole thing appeared an utter mockery. To unskilled men, the work of clearing seemed

181

hopeless; they were naturally afraid of the Red Indian and of the wild beasts of the forest; without roads or paths, they were frightened to move for fear of getting lost.

Can we wonder that, in such circumstances, they refused to settle on the company's lands? Though, in consequence, when provisions arrived, the agents refused to give them any. Ross and the company quarrelled, and he ultimately left the newcomers to their fate. The few of them who had a little money bought what provisions they could from the agents, while others, less fortunate, exchanged their clothes for food, but the greater number had neither money nor clothes to spend or exchange and they were all soon left quite destitute. Thus driven to extremity, they determined to have the provisions retained by the agents, right or wrong, and two of them went to claim them. They were refused but they determined to take what they could by force.

They seized the agents, tied them, took their guns from them, which they hid at a distance; they told them that they must have the food for their families, but that they were quite willing and determined to pay for them if ever they were able to do so. They then carefully weighed or measured the various articles, took account of what each man received and left, except one, a powerful and determined fellow who was left behind to release the two agents. This he did after allowing sufficient time for his friends to get to a safe distance, when he informed the prisoners where they could find their guns. Intelligence was sent to Halifax that the Highlanders were in rebellion, from whence orders were sent to a Captain Archibald in Truro, to march his company of militia to suppress and pacify them but, to his honour, be it said, he sent word that he would do no such thing. 'I know the Highlanders,' he said, 'and if they are fairly treated there will be no trouble with them.' Finally, orders were given to supply them with provisions, and Mr. Paterson, one of the agents, used afterwards to say that the Highlanders who arrived in poverty, and who had been so badly treated, had paid him every farthing with which he had trusted them.

It would be tedious to describe the sufferings which they afterwards endured. Many of them left. Others, fathers, mothers and children, bound themselves away, as virtual slaves, in other settlements, for mere subsistence. Those who remained lived in small huts, covered only with the bark of branches of trees to shelter them from the bitter winter cold, of the severity of which they had no previous conception. They had to walk some eighty miles, through a trackless forest, in deep snow to Truro, to obtain a few bushels of potatoes, or a little flour in exchange for their labour, dragging these back all the way again on their backs, and endless cases of great suffering from actual want occurred. The remembrance of these terrible days sank deep into the minds of that generation, and long after, even to this day, the narration of the scenes and cruel hardships through which they had to pass beguiled, and now beguiles many a winter's night as they sit by their now comfortable firesides.

In the following spring they set to work. They cleared some of the forest, and planted a larger crop. They learned to hunt moose. They began to cut timber and sent a cargo of it from Pictou – the first of a trade carried on profitably and extensively since. The population now amounted only to 78 persons. One of the modes of laying up a supply of food for the winter was to dig up a large quantity of clams, pile them in heaps on the seashore and then cover them over with sand, though they were often, in winter, obliged to cut through ice more than a foot thick to get at them.

In Prince Edward Island, a colony from Lockerbie, in Dumfriesshire, who came out in 1774, seemed to have fared even worse. They commenced operations on the Island with fair prospects of success, when a plague of locusts or field mice broke out and consumed everything, even the potatoes in the ground. For eighteen months the settlers experienced all the miseries of a famine, having for several months only what lobsters or shellfish they could gather from the seashore. The winter brought them to such a state of weakness that they were unable to convey food a reasonable distance even when they had means to buy it.

In this pitiful position, they heard that the Pictou people were making progress that year and that they had even some provisions to spare. Fifteen families left for the earlier settlement, where, for a time, they fared little better, but afterwards became prosperous and happy. A few of their children and thousands of their grandchildren are now living in comfort and plenty.

But who can think of these early hardships without condemning the memories of the heartless Highland and Scottish lairds who made existence at home almost as miserable for those noble fellows and who then drove them in thousands out of their native land, not caring whether they sank in the Atlantic or were starved to death on a strange and uncongenial soil? Retributive justice demands that posterity should execrate the memories of the authors of such horrid cruelty. It may seem uncharitable to write thus of the dead, but it is impossible to forget their inhuman conduct, though, no thanks to them, it has turned out for the better for the descendants of those who were banished to what was then infinitely worse than transportation for the worst crimes. Such criminals were looked after and cared for but those poor fellows, driven out of their homes by the Highland lairds and sent across there, were left to starve, helpless and uncared for. Their descendants are now a prosperous and thriving people. The descendants of the evicted from Sutherland, Ross, Inverness-shire and elsewhere to Canada, are producing enormous quantities of food and millions of cattle, to pour them into this country. What will be the consequence? The sheep farmer – the original cause of the evictions – will be the first to suffer. The price of stock in Scotland must inevitably fall. Rents must follow, and the joint authors of the original iniquity will, as a class, then suffer the natural and just penalty of their past misconduct.

An Evicting Agent

Giving evidence before the Deer Forest Commission of 1892, the late Mr. Eneas R. Macdonell of Camusdarroch, Arisaig, made an interesting statement. After mentioning that he was a member of the Scottish Bar, and had previously been proprietor of Morar, he proceeded:

'I am able to speak generally as to the population there used to be in Arisaig in my young days – in fact, the whole tract of country seemed to be populated and to have numerous houses on all parts of it, but I want to confine my evidence almost entirely to that portion of the district which is now under deer forest. It is now called Rhu–Arisaig but, one hundred years ago, it was called Dubh-chamus.

'Although I am only seventy-two years of age, I am able to speak of thirty years beyond that, from 1794. My grandfather occupied the various places or townships in Dubh–chamus or Rudha. I am able to speak concerning that period from an old account-book belonging to my grandfather, to which I had access a good many years ago, and it was in connection with a very melancholy occasion in which I was unfortunately implicated, viz., an emigration from the estate of Loch Sheil in Moidart. In that account-book, I found thirty-seven names of individuals in the various families who were paying rent, as sub-tenants to my grandfather, Archibald Macdonald, Rudha, Arisaig, who died in 1828 or 1829. At that time the account-book was in the possession of my uncle, Macdonald of Loch Sheil. It was in connection with Rudha that I came to examine the book.

'First I should mention that these people occupied Rhu as cottars and they had land for which apparently they paid no rent, but worked the land, of which Mr. Macdonald of Rudha cropped a portion. They paid a nominal rent for grazing and he himself paid a very small rent also to the then proprietor, Macdonald of Clanranald. In fact he, as well as Macdonald of Borrodale and Macdonald of Glen Alladale, came into possession of the various lands as being sons of the then Macdonald of Clanranald. They took these lands with the population on them, and occupied them.

'The rents were paid to the tenants, to these Macdonalds, at a very small rate because they themselves were not highly charged.

'It so came to pass that, in Lord Cranston's time, my uncle, Gregor Macdonald, who then occupied Rudha, had to give a large increase of rent or be quit of it. Well, he could not under the old system on which he held it afford to give more rent. The consequence was that the farm was taken over him. The cruel thing was that he was obliged to remove all the sub-tenants upon it, who had been there genera-

185

tions before him or his ancestors. The only thing that he could do was to get his brother Macdonald of Loch Sheil to take the people over to Loch Sheil in Moidart. Times grew black and the potato famine occurred. The consequence was that there was a redundant population, for Moidart had previously been well inhabited and the addition of so many families from Rudha, Arisaig, quite overwhelmed them when the potato famine occurred.

'I was then puzzled to know how many came from Rudha, Arisaig, and I got access in that way to the old books, where I found a list of names of the people and the portions of Rudha that they occupied. These are in all thirty-seven and they are evidently of different families. The rents were given and the payments made, and everything in connection with their holdings. The date of this is 1794.

'I was going on to explain that these people, or rather the descendants of some of them, had to be removed to Moidart and, in the congested state of the estate, it had to be considered what was best to be done. I was then a young man. I had just passed at the Bar, and I and the late respected James Macgregor of Fort William were appointed trustees to do what was best. We could see nothing for it but to assist them to emigrate and we were assisted materially in carrying out the emigration by the resident Catholic clergyman of that time, Rev. Ronald Rankine, who followed them. So many of them went to Australia and a few of them to America. But never shall I forget until my dying day. It is a source of grief to me that I had anything whatsoever to do with that emigration, although, at the same time, God knows I cannot understand how it could have been averted. Many of the people have succeeded and are well-to-do but, if they had remained, they would have been impoverished themselves, and they would have impoverished the few that are still on the estate.'